PITTSBURGH'S
LOST OUTPOST

PITTSBURGH'S
LOST OUTPOST

Captain Trent's Fort

JASON A. CHERRY

Foreword by David L. Preston

THE
History
PRESS

Published by The History Press
Charleston, SC
www.historypress.com

First published 2019

Manufactured in the United States

ISBN 9781467141628

Library of Congress Control Number: 2018963529

In memory of my second father and the commander of Captain William Trent's Company, Jack Oelschlager, who for almost thirty years taught me how to immerse myself in eighteenth-century life.

CONTENTS

FOREWORD

William Trent's life was indelibly shaped by a world at war, and Trent in turn shaped many of its key moments. He participated in every major conflict of the mid-eighteenth century, and his military career is notable for how often he was defending forts. During King George's War (1744–48), he was a company commander of Pennsylvania provincials, leading them northward to New York, where they defended a fort at Saratoga. As a Pennsylvania trader, he was among the advent of British traders in the Ohio Valley who threatened French alliances and trade, prompting the French military to invade and control the region. From 1753 to 1754, Trent was at the tip of the spear of the Ohio Company, participating in diplomacy with Ohio Country natives and orchestrating the movements of men and supplies to secure the strategic Forks of the Ohio. He later participated in John Forbes's expedition in 1758, which finally expelled the French from Fort Duquesne and aided in the defense of Fort Pitt during Pontiac's War in 1763. Trent's involvements in the French and Indian War and Pontiac's War were truly significant, placing him alongside George Washington, George Croghan, Robert Dinwiddie, John Forbes and other notable players in that history.

It is Trent's pivotal role in the initial 1754 British fort at the Forks of the Ohio—variously called Trent's Fort or Fort Prince George—that is the focus of this book. For many years, Sewell Elias Slick's *William Trent and the West*, published in 1947, has been the only biographical work on Trent's notable life in the eighteenth century. Jason Cherry's work explores Trent's role at the

Forks of the Ohio with greater detail and with newer sources. In addition, it situates the reader in Trent's life through photographic documentation of the places where Trent once trod. Mr. Cherry also brings to this study a lifelong commitment to the study and preservation of eighteenth-century history. The result is a story that illuminates William Trent's role in Britain's westward expansion and the origins of a small British outpost that would ultimately become Fort Pitt, in turn giving rise to the city of Pittsburgh.

PROFESSOR DAVID PRESTON,
The Citadel

ACKNOWLEDGEMENTS

After all the research and planning for this book, I couldn't imagine beginning without recognizing the special people who made this possible.

First and foremost, I want to acknowledge my parents. Without their love of history and passion to educate others, I would not be where I am today. It was their guidance that provided the spark to learn about history and attention to detail that got me interested. I cannot also thank enough my brother Justin, whose drive for research about this period and fresh pair of eyes helped me shape the true nature of this story.

This leads me to this next group of people, about which I can clearly say without hesitation is my second family. For almost thirty years, my living history unit, Captain William Trent's Company, was my transportation back into the eighteenth century and the reason I chose William Trent as my central figure in the book.

Countless thanks go to my good friend Professor David Preston, whose advice and feedback was so helpful since the day we discussed his book in the works about General Braddock many years ago when we met reenacting at Fort Loudon in Tennessee.

The same can be said about Erica Nuckles, the director of history and collections at Fort Ligonier. She was so vital in assisting me any way that she could, and I can say it has been a blessing to know her since we were kids reenacting with our units at various historic sites.

The next person I want to recognize, Fred Threlfall, possessed knowledge of this specific period that was key to providing accurate details and anecdotes, including being the one who first made me aware of "Trent's Remarks," located at the University of Michigan. His amazing artwork was also a key contribution to this story becoming a reality.

Speaking of the University of Michigan, I cannot thank enough the staff over the years at William L. Clements Library who helped me with the Trent's Remarks manuscript and made sure that this document was given its proper recognition. This document filled in the gaps of my timeline that had been missing since Trent first began trekking to the Forks of the Ohio.

This timeline took a great deal of research, and to show Trent's route to the Forks of the Ohio for the first time on a digital map, I must thank the staff at Mapping Specialists Inc. out of Fitchburg, Wisconsin. Both Don Larson and Glen Pawelski did a tremendous job in ensuring that the Trent map was everything I hoped it would accomplish visually.

Another great place and group of people I want to acknowledge are at the William Trent House and the William Trent House Association. Bringing the William Trent vest out of their archives to let me personally view it made the reality of William Trent come off the pages, as I could picture him wearing this while scribing his letters from England.

For the original letters and documents in Trent's hand and the discovery of his parents' original marriage certificate, I want to thank the Historical Society of Pennsylvania in Philadelphia. All the staff were most helpful getting the marriage certificate digitalized for the first time and assisting me with what I feel is the greatest collection of William Trent documents out there.

I must also thank Fort Necessity National Battlefield and park interpreter Brian Reedy for his exclusive knowledge about the battle, including the aftermath of those slain relating to the new details found in Trent's Remarks.

In addition, there is the painting *Arrival of the French*, beautifully done by Pittsburgh native Nat Youngblood in 1969. I am thankful for use of this accurate depiction by the painting's owner, Robert MacLachlan, and the further promotion of Mr. Youngblood's portrayal of early events throughout Western Pennsylvania. Another artist I would like to extend my gratitude to is Robert Griffing. His accurate depictions of Native Americans and eighteenth-century life are why I chose to use his painting *Half King and Trent at the Forks* for the book's front cover. Also included with him is Gerald Seymour of Paramount Press, who provided me the use of Griffing's beautiful artwork.

Finally, my publisher, The History Press, decided graciously to take a chance on my book and allow Trent's untold story of his fort in the early years of Pittsburgh to be showcased all over.

Last but certainly not least, I must thank my beautiful wife, Emily, and our children, Penny and Charlotte. Their love and support made it possible to be both a great father and author. Emily, my heart and my rock, thank you for supporting me and understanding as I made you and the kids stop at every historical museum and marker that I felt was relevant in telling of Trent's story. I could not have done any of this without you by my side.

Sir: In regard to Captain Trent; Mr Mercer did Receive from Governor Dinwiddie a Sum of Money but what sum I know not, whatever the Sum was I am apt to believe it was for Goods belonging to the Ohio Company Except what was due him—as Captain of a Company four or five months as he was directed by Dinwooddie [sic] to Build a Fort at the Mouth of the Monongahalia and not being furnished with money by the Governor he was obliged to make use of the Company's money as well as Goods Such as Blankets, Guns, Powder, Lead &c to pay the Workman and furnish them with Provisions for that Purpose as appears in the Company's Books Charged to the Government of Virginia and Fort St. George so called in the Company's Books.

—Thomas Cresap to James Tilghman III on May 20, 1767

Introduction

LOST HISTORY

In November 2008, the city of Pittsburgh celebrated its 250th birthday. It was an incredible milestone recognizing the rich history of a city traditionally known for its steel mills and passionate sport teams. Yet growing up in Western Pennsylvania, I was astonished to find out that the humble beginnings of Pittsburgh truly began when a group of English traders began constructing an outpost at the "Point" in early spring of 1754.

The Point was a triangular piece of land that rested at the confluence of the Allegheny and Monongahela Rivers, forming the Ohio River. Known simply as the Forks of the Ohio, the navigable waterways were extremely valuable to the French, who needed this location to control the Ohio Valley from the St. Lawrence River to the Mississippi River. For the British, it was the center to control not only the booming fur trade (which heavily influenced the native people in the Ohio Country) but also westward expansion of the British empire across America.

The person trusted to proceed with this mission to the Forks of the Ohio in the winter of 1754 was former soldier turned trader William Trent. Trent, who had left the thriving business world of Philadelphia[1] behind for the untamed wilderness in the Ohio Valley, accepted without hesitation. He attempted to stake Britain's claim throughout the Ohio Country by first recruiting traders and men from Virginia. Unfortunately, what happened over the next four months at the Forks of the Ohio would prompt the eventual opening shots of the French and Indian War.

Despite such an important event situated around the future site of Pittsburgh, the real story of what happened was seemingly lost or forgotten over time. To make matters worse, most scholarly books written about the French and Indian War tend to skip over this specific event involving Trent or mention it only as a glorified footnote.

While doing my research of the first outpost built at the Forks of the Ohio by Captain William Trent and his men in the spring of 1754, I understood why such details were not well known or just lost. Firsthand accounts concerning these early months of 1754 were rare. Even those few primary sources actually found gave little or no intimate details of William Trent or his men.

Fortunately, after meticulous research, this book solves the mystery of Pittsburgh's lost outpost and sheds light on the influential character known as William Trent.

Chapter 1

THE BEGINNING

The struggle for the Ohio Valley in the 1750s had its roots more than a century earlier, in the 1609 Charter of Virginia. By 1744, Virginians had expanded over the Blue Ridge and were looking toward the Ohio Valley. It was the Treaty of Lancaster in 1744 that set the pieces in motion. As was discussed in this treaty and stipulated in the 1609 Charter, "land granted was from sea to sea, west and northwest." Based on that original generalized claim to the Virginia Company[2] by James I,[3] it ceded the lands west of the Ohio River unbeknownst to the Six Nations[4] and gave Thomas Lee,[5] a Northern Neck[6] proprietor, opportunity to propose a prosperous land scheme. Recognizing the potential of the Ohio Country for colonization, Thomas Lee in 1747 joined other Northern Neck proprietors Augustine Washington[7] and Lawrence Washington[8] to form a land speculation company called the Ohio Company. Their goal was to represent the trading interests of Virginia investors while looking to extend the dominion of Great Britain deeper in North America.

Two years later, in 1749, they did just that, after the British Crown granted the Ohio Company 500,000 acres in the Ohio Valley between the Kanawha[9] and the Monongahela Rivers.[10] The grant, however, came in two parts. The first part, being the first 200,000 acres, was to be promised, with the next 300,000 acres granted only if the Ohio Company successfully settled one hundred families within seven years[11] and built a fort at its own expense to protect these settlers. To further promote settlement, these settlers could live on this land rent and tax free for ten years.

So, where does one start if he wants people to purchase this land? Because the 200,000 acres in the upper and lower Ohio Country were mostly rivers and uncharted wilderness, the Ohio Company assigned Indian trader and surveyor Christopher Gist[12] to explore these lands. He would make two different trips into the Ohio Country, the first trip from October 31, 1750, to May 19, 1751, and the second trip from November 4, 1751, to March 29, 1752.[13] His careful, detailed observations of timber, native villages and trade would be most helpful to those willing to eventually settle on their purchased lots.

Portrait of Ohio Company founder Thomas Lee. *Courtesy of the author.*

Yet on May 28, 1752, it became apparent at the council of Logstown[14] between British commissioners and the Six Nations that the Ohio Company was not the only one showing valued interest in the Ohio Country.

In 1749, Céloron de Blainville[15] led a party of French troops down the Belle Riviere, burying lead plates[16] along their route to renew French claims to the region.

To make matters worse, the Iroquois viceroy[17] named Tanarisson, or the "Half King,"[18] argued that the Six Nations had not ceded land beyond the Allegheny Mountains in the Treaty of Lancaster of 1744 but did promise to not molest or harass any English settlements southeast of the Ohio River. Tanarisson[19] resided in Logstown on the banks of the Ohio River, eighteen miles below the Forks, and despite his bitterness, he did make one formal request: he wished the English would build a fort at the mouth of the Monongahela.[20]

Unfortunately, by the fall of 1753, two French forts and one supply post had been constructed. The first, at Lake Erie, was named Fort Presque Isle,[21] the second to the south was Fort Le Boeuf.[22] The one supply post was aptly named Venango,[23] while the English had still not built any outposts throughout what is known today as Western Pennsylvania.

This French invasion became too much for not only King George II[24] but also the lieutenant governor of Virginia and prominent shareholder in the Ohio Company Robert Dinwiddie.[25] Asserting the claim of the Ohio Company, Dinwiddie needed someone to travel hundreds of miles through

The Half King or Tanarisson, by Fred Threlfall. *Courtesy of Fred Threlfall.*

Left: Christopher Gist, by Fred Threlfall. *Courtesy of Fred Threlfall.*

Right: George Washington, by Rembrandt Peale, circa 1820–50. *Courtesy of Fort Ligonier in Ligonier, Pennsylvania.*

perilous wilderness to deliver a formal message to the French commandant and warn him against trespassing on Britain's claim to lands north of Logstown and in the upper Ohio Country. For this arduous journey of importance, the governor and his council selected a young adjutant and former surveyor for Lord Fairfax[26] who had volunteered for the mission. The emissary they selected on October 27, 1753,[27] was also the younger brother of Lawrence Washington and virtually an unknown at the time. The name of this young man who entered the history books was George Washington.[28]

Chapter 2

EARLY PREPARATION

O n November 23, 1753, George Washington, the ambitious twenty-one-year-old surveyor, stood studying the landscape with his hired guide, Christopher Gist. The mouth of the Monongahela left him in awe, the sheer sight of it provoking a rather thoughtful description:[29]

> *As I had taken a good deal of Notice Yesterday of the Situation at the Forks,*[30] *my Curiosity led me to examine this more particularly, and I think it is greatly inferior either for Defence or Advantages; especially the latter; for a Fort at the Forks would be equally well situated on Ohio, and have the entire Command of Monongahela, which runs up to our Settlements and is extremely well design'd for Water carriage, as it is of a deep still Nature, besides a fort at the Forks might be built at a much less Expence, than at the other place.*

This "other" place Washington was referring to, of course, was on the southeast side of the River Ohio[31] near the mouth of Chartier's Creek,[32] the place noted on George Mercer's[33] map in 1753 that he named Fort Hill:

> *This Hill is a very fine Situation for a Fort, being very steep on North and South Sides and River running at the Foot of it on the North Side, as it does at the East End which is inaccessible, being near 100 Feet high and large Rocks jutting one over the other to the Top. The West End has a gradual Descent down to the River.*[34]

Present-day view of the Ohio River from Point State Park in Pittsburgh, Pennsylvania, and what Major George Washington saw when he first arrived at the Forks of the Ohio in November 1753. *Courtesy of the author.*

This was also the initial site the landholding agency the Ohio Company had proposed to build on when the committee had met on July 25, 1753. At this meeting, the committee chose three individuals to oversee the potential fort who had been both Indian traders by occupation and employees of the

The first suggested site for the Ohio Company fort on Chartier's Creek called "Fort Hill" and surveyed by George Mercer in 1753. It was located on the McKees Rocks Indian Mound in McKees Rocks, Pennsylvania. *Courtesy of the author.*

Ohio Company. For supervision of the laborers, carpenters and workmen, they chose Thomas Cresap, Christopher Gist and William Trent.

Thomas Cresap, who lived in "Skipton,"[35] Maryland, was notorious for his brutal encounters as a former agent of Lord Baltimore[36] during the Maryland-Pennsylvania border conflict. He not only worked as an itinerant for the Ohio Company, but he was also a shareholding member.

Christopher Gist, a former resident of the Yadkin River Valley[37] in North Carolina and who then had residences at Will's Creek[38] and at the foot of Laurel Hill,[39] needed no introduction from his surveying services and exploration of the upper and lower Ohio Country from 1750 to 1752.

The third individual, William Trent, would powerfully embrace the true embodiment of the Ohio Company's plan. Trent had earned a captain's commission when he commanded a company of one hundred Pennsylvanians during King George's War from 1746 to 1747,[40] and he had the most distinguished lineage of the three. His father, former Supreme Court justice William Trent,[41] was one of the wealthiest merchants in Philadelphia and whose surname was the namesake for the settlement of Trent's Town,[42] New Jersey. His mother, Mary Coddington Trent,[43] was the stepdaughter of

Location of Christopher Gist's plantation or Gist's settlement in 1754 and today in Mount Braddock, Pennsylvania. The Isaac Meason House on the hill, completed in 1802, resides currently where the house of Christopher Gist once stood. *Courtesy of the author.*

Quaker Anthony Morris,[44] the second mayor of Philadelphia and founder of Morris Brewery.

Although no sculptures or paintings of Trent are known to exist, there is one piece of evidence that gives us clues as to Trent's measurements and how he stood up in comparison to the tall-in-stature George Washington.

The William Trent House—the oldest building in Trenton, New Jersey,[45] and original 1719 residence of his father, Justice William Trent—recently had in its archival collections an original vest gifted by the former Trent Chapter of the Daughters of the American Revolution (DAR) at the Old Barracks from Miss Anna Rossell on November 12, 1905. Miss Rossell was the great-granddaughter of Captain William Trent and had said that the original vest or waistcoat in her possession was one her ancestor had worn in 1769 when he traveled to England to address the Court of St. James for losses suffered in 1754 and 1763 by traders of the Ohio Company.

On September 28, 1978, the article of clothing was sent to the textile conservator at the Winterthur Museum in Delaware for closer examination,

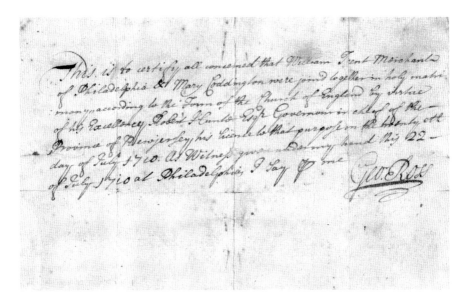

Marriage certificate of Captain Trent's parents, William Trent and Mary Coddington, dated July 20, 1710. *Courtesy of the Historical Society of Pennsylvania in Philadelphia, Pennsylvania.*

The William Trent House, built in 1719 in Trenton, New Jersey. *Courtesy of the author.*

Close-up of the woof and warp patterns on the buttons of Trent's vest, dated 1769. *Courtesy of the William Trent House Association.*

and the results were nothing short of remarkable. The vest was warped and woofed[46] woven silk, and what was at first thought to be blue flower embroidery down the buttoned front edges and along the sides horizontally at the hem was concluded to be woven silk threads wrapped in silver foil to give the fancy metallic appearance. It was a popular height of fashion at the time, and given that Trent was a man of gentleman status, the coat was tight fitting to his body and tailor made, thus detailing for the first time accurate measurements to his apparent size.

The neck was measured first and was calculated as being just short of 15¾ inches. Next, the waist was measured and was recorded as being 33 or 34 in waist size, a rather average build for the period. But surprisingly, the front and back of the coat were measured lengthwise, and it was determined that Trent had a rather long torso, about 25 inches. Now, a long torso does not always dictate height, but comparing these numbers to a waistcoat made in 1776 for George Washington, who stood around 6 feet, 2½ inches,[47] and the numbers are fairly close. The Smithsonian lists Washington's circa 1776 silk coat as 26⅜ inches long by 21 inches wide, while Trent's coat was almost 25 inches long and about 22 inches wide. Since we know that Washington had a tall frame with long legs, it can be estimated for the first time after neck-to-waist ratio configurations that William Trent stood almost 6 feet, 1 inch tall.

After the three supervisors were named, the Ohio Company projected a fort and a town to be called Saltsburg, to encourage the settling of German Protestants. It was envisioned to be "twelve feet high to be built of sawed and hewed logs and to include a piece of ground ninety feet square besides the four bastions at the corners of sixteen feet square each with houses in the middle for stores, magazines."[48]

Unfortunately, all these proposed ideas were just wishful thinking by the Ohio Company for the time being. At the meeting of the Executive Council of Virginia on August 24, 1753, Governor Robert Dinwiddie announced a

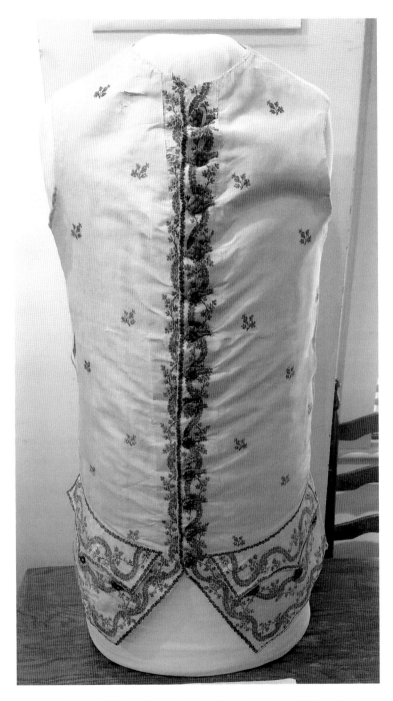

The vest of Major William Trent, dated 1769. *Courtesy of the William Trent House Association.*

letter in his possession dated August 11 from William Trent, noting that "the French whose army consists of about one thousand five hundred soldiers from old France, within three months will have three forts on the Ohio River, that they declare publicly they have all the land as far as Allegheny Hill[49] and will build Towns and Forts where they please."[50] William Fairfax,[51] the president of the Governor's Council, announced at this meeting that "another letter from Mr. Trent intimated the great desire of the Indians to see the Governor of Virginia," especially the chosen "voice" of the Six Nations, Tanarisson.

When Tanarisson spoke to Trent on July 16, 1753, he was extremely embittered by his previous visit to the French commandant[52] at Fort Le Boeuf. Trent had said that "the Half King informed him that he had heard the French General say that he was coming down Ohio to take possession of it. That he would call at the Forks and ask the English what they were doing there and bid them go off and if they did not go they would catch them by the Hair and beat them." The Half King also said, "The French General said he was now coming to build as low as the mouth of Beaver Creek[53] as that one part of his People was coming down Scioto[54] and up Ohio till they met."

In other words, while one month had already passed since that initial meeting in July between the Half King and Trent, the colony of Virginia had to act quickly. William Fairfax, however, made a motion to approve "a commission appointing Capt. Trent to command a Body of Rangers may be of service."[55]

It might have heightened the race to obtain possession of the Ohio Valley for Great Britain had the Governor's Council approved of Trent's commission, instead of waiting on official orders from London to proceed into the Ohio Country. After all, William Trent was a veteran captain of King George's War and was battle tested, after being ambushed by French and Indians on April 7, 1747,[56] near Old Fort Saratoga.[57] Despite being one of several French and Indian raids across the New York frontier, the skirmish proved to be an unforgettable one for Trent. That day not only had he lost his baggage[58] to the enemy, but one of his soldiers captured as a prisoner also mistakenly identified Trent as one of the eight who perished in the battle.[59]

Trent's academic prowess was also the reason why he was suggested or mentioned among the governor's council. Before his venture into the military, he also had been trained as a merchant's apprentice in Philadelphia. He would learn his trade by keeping books for the firm of prominent merchants James Logan and his maternal great-uncle by marriage, Edward Shippen,[60]

Grave of Trent's mentor Edward Shippen III at St. James Episcopal Church Cemetery in Lancaster, Pennsylvania. *Courtesy of the author.*

in Philadelphia from about the mid-1730s to about 1744.[61] Primary evidence throughout his lifetime also suggests that Trent was well versed in not only writing English grammar but also in Latin exercises and phrases.[62] Trent may have received a rudimentary understanding of surveying from Edward Shippen, a founder of the College of New Jersey,[63] who was also a proverbial scholar in the French language and the art of trigonometry,[64] before he left Shippen's firm and bought his first piece of land trading in Lancaster County, Pennsylvania, in 1745.[65] Later, in 1753, when he resided on the North Branch of the Potomac River, Trent would be a district justice in Frederick County, Virginia.[66]

Unfortunately, the commission would have to wait a few months for Trent as he explored and viewed the chosen site of the Ohio Company fort with John Fraser[67] and the "half breed" Andrew Montour.[68] Fraser was a Scottish gunsmith and had been a trader at Venango[69] since 1741, only to be forced from his post from the French. He resettled at a small cabin at the junction of Turtle Creek[70] and the Monongahela River. The house was just eight miles from the Forks of the Ohio, and in a letter written to his business partner, James Young,[71] dated August 27, 1753, Fraser noted, "Captain Trent was here the night before last and viewed the ground the fort was to be built on. They will begin in less than a month's time."

Trent was observing in August the new future site of the Ohio Company fort, preceding by three months what young Major Washington would also observe as he and Gist rode by on their journey north to Fort Le Boeuf in November 1753.

Now Trent and Governor Dinwiddie knew that the fort's construction would ultimately depend on the support of local natives. So, with Dinwiddie's suggestion, Trent would offer weapons, ammunition and other sundry items like clothes and wampum, but only if the Six Nations allowed them to build a "strong house" at the Forks of the Ohio. It was a provocative bribe to those ninety-eight Native Americans who arrived in Winchester on September 10, 1753, especially since the Half King was not present.[72] In fact, the Half King held nothing back when describing the true intentions of the French in his letter to those present at the treaty: "I tell you a glass of liquor is a Frenchman's hatchet for while you are thinking you are with your friend, he basely poisoning you, the way he has served several of us and intended to do to me, but I know them and wanted to drink none with them."[73]

The Half King also suggested to Governor Dinwiddie that he feared "a great part of the Six Nations do favor the French and said most settlers already on Ohio Company lands will be obliged to move off if the Governor

Right: Portrait of Virginia lieutenant governor and Ohio Company shareholder Robert Dinwiddie. *Courtesy of the National Portrait Gallery.*

Below: Viewpoint from the mouth of French Creek at Riverfront Park in Franklin, Pennsylvania—also the supposed site of John Fraser's cabin, 1741–53. *Courtesy of the author.*

doesn't find some method speedily to stop the progress of the French."[74] These words must have alarmed the governor. Besides being the acting lieutenant governor of Virginia, he also was a prominent member of the Ohio Company, and the last thing he wanted was the Indians and settlers opposing Ohio Company claims even before a fort could be built at the Forks of the Ohio.

So, Dinwiddie hatched a plan to spy on the newly built French outposts to verify their true intentions and still protect the interests of the Ohio Company. With the Executive Council, he chose the young adjutant George Washington, who volunteered from the Southern District,[75] to venture to the commandant of the French forces to learn by what authority they presumed to make encroachments on His Majesty's lands on the Ohio. It was a dangerous mission. If the expendable Washington were killed, it would only justify the British view that the French and their Indian allies were only there to trespass and murder.[76] The diplomatic mission also masked the Virginians' real motive, which was to control the Ohio Valley just as strongly as the French were currently controlling it.

Dinwiddie probably suspected what the French reply to his summons would be even before sending an emissary northward. It was already presumed that they weren't leaving, especially since hearing William Trent's previous report of the aftermath of the burning of Pickawillany in 1752[77] and the recent influx of French arriving at Logstown.

So, without waiting for Washington's return, Dinwiddie dispatched a carriage of presents such as powder, lead and flints, as well as other sundry gifts, for William Trent, who left Winchester, Virginia,[78] and arrived at Colonel Thomas Cresap's house in Shawnee Old Town, Maryland. The intent of this carriage was to deliver these presents to the chiefs of the Six Nations as Dinwiddie had promised, at which time Colonel William Fairfax read the governor's speech to them on September 11, 1753.

Yet as the hours grew thinner and with British patience with the Six Nations rapidly dwindling, it was William Trent, the appointed factor of the Ohio Company,[79] who made the first bold move. Even without receiving any official orders from the Virginia government to advance, Trent recruited twenty artificers[80] at the Inhabitants, just across the North Branch of the Potomac, and sent them on their way into the upper Ohio Country with supplies he deemed necessary.

To say that these twenty men were rugged was an understatement. Mostly backwoodsmen without proper soldier's attire, these fortunate souls chosen by Trent were skillful former freelancing employees of the Ohio Company

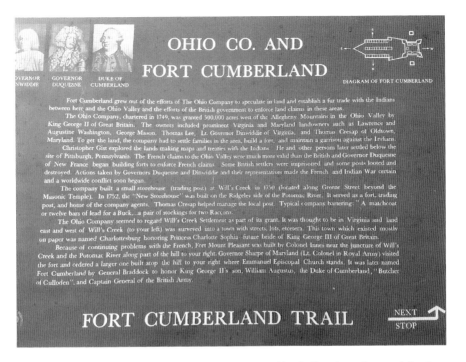

OHIO CO. AND FORT CUMBERLAND

DIAGRAM OF FORT CUMBERLAND

Fort Cumberland grew out of the efforts of The Ohio Company to speculate in land and establish a fur trade with the Indians between here and the Ohio Valley and the efforts of the British government to enforce land claims in these areas.

The Ohio Company, chartered in 1749, was granted 500,000 acres west of the Allegheny Mountains in the Ohio Valley by King George II of Great Britain. The owners included prominent Virginia and Maryland landowners such as Lawrence and Augustine Washington, George Mason, Thomas Lee, Lt. Governor Dinwiddie of Virginia, and Thomas Cresap of Oldtown, Maryland. To get the land, the company had to settle families in the area, build a fort, and maintain a garrison against the Indians.

Christopher Gist explored the lands making maps and treaties with the Indians. He and other persons later settled below the site of Pittsburgh, Pennsylvania. The French claims to the Ohio Valley were much more valid than the British and Governor Duquesne of New France began building forts to enforce French claims. Some British settlers were imprisoned and some posts looted and destroyed. Actions taken by Governors Duquesne and Dinwiddie and their representatives made the French and Indian War certain and a worldwide conflict soon began.

The company built a small storehouse (trading post) at Will's Creek in 1750 (located along Greene Street beyond the Masonic Temple). In 1752, the "New Storehouse" was built on the Ridgeley side of the Potomac River. It served as a fort, trading post, and home of the company agents. Thomas Cresap helped manage the local post. Typical company bartering: "A matchcoat or twelve bars of lead for a Buck,...a pair of stockings for two Raccons."

The Ohio Company seemed to regard Will's Creek Settlement as part of its grant. It was thought to be in Virginia and land east and west of Will's Creek (to your left) was surveyed into a town with streets, lots, etcetera. This town which existed mostly on paper was named Charlottesburg honoring Princess Charlotte Sophia future bride of King George III of Great Britain.

Because of continuing problems with the French, Fort Mount Pleasant was built by Colonel Innes near the juncture of Will's Creek and the Potomac River along part of the hill to your right. Governor Sharpe of Maryland (Lt. Colonel in Royal Army) visited the fort and ordered a larger one built atop the hill to your right where Emmanuel Episcopal Church stands. It was later named Fort Cumberland by General Braddock to honor King George II's son, William Augustus, the Duke of Cumberland, "Butcher of Culloden", and Captain-General of the British Army.

FORT CUMBERLAND TRAIL   NEXT STOP

Historical sign commemorating the Ohio Company and its dealings in and around the site of Fort Cumberland. *Courtesy of the author.*

and, coincidentally, also the same men whom Major Washington and Christopher Gist would encounter on January 6, 1754, before they arrived at Will's Creek.

On that same day, Trent delivered a letter to George Washington, who personally handed it to Governor Dinwiddie on January 16, 1754, upon his return to Williamsburg. Although this letter has never been found, Dinwiddie noted Trent's words from it in another letter dated January 26, 1754, in which he quoted Trent as saying "that if properly impower'd to do so, he would stop the French advance during the winter." It was impeccable timing, though, considering that unbeknownst to both of them, a few hundred French militia and regulars had already left Quebec on January 15, 1754, and had begun their cold and icy trek south to the Ohio Country.

The words were powerful nonetheless, and their strong ambition would seduce Dinwiddie more than he thought. For in a few weeks, the governor of Virginia would also make a bold move of his own.

Chapter 3

A CONVENIENT PLACE

O n January 6, 1754, as Washington's mission was almost concluding, another new mission began when "seventeen horses were loaded with materials and stores for a fort at the Forks"[81] that day. Now, it was known through Washington's journal that it was just him and Christopher Gist, but who was leading the other party that he wrote had met them a day out from the Inhabitants? Despite little primary evidence to capture Trent's timeline to the Ohio Country, many scholars assumed that William Trent was traveling with those twenty artificers because of the letter dated January 6, 1754, from William Trent to Governor Dinwiddie that he had given to Washington, but this is incorrect. In fact, it could be said that if someone as notable as William Trent traveled past, Washington or Gist would not have failed to mention seeing him on the sixth in his diary entries. So was there another reason behind Gist and Washington not referencing specifically Trent leading the caravan of artificers?

Let's closely examine the description in Washington's journal entry on January 6, 1754, when he said that "he saw seventeen horses were loaded," instead of saying, "Mr. Trent or Capt. Trent and seventeen horses were loaded with materials and stores for a fort at the Forks." It is quite possible then that Trent was not with them yet. Fortunately, for the first time in publication, the true answer can finally be revealed to confirm the disputed timeline of Trent's whereabouts.

In 2002, the William L. Clements Library at the University of Michigan–Ann Arbor acquired a document written by William Trent, his remarks in response to the French book *A Memorial Containing a Summary View of Facts, with Their Authorities in Answer to the Observations Sent by the English Ministry to the Courts of Europe* by Jacob Nicolas Moreau.

Written in what was most likely late summer of 1757, Trent's Remarks, as I refer to them in this book, contain valuable new details on the events of 1754. The first of such passages was the exact date of when Trent left the Inhabitants, and it was not January 6 with the twenty artificers. He wrote:

> *On the 21 January 1754 I left my own house near where Fort Cumberland now stands with a quantity of Powder, Lead and Flints sent by the Governor of Virginia to the Indians at their repeated request to defend themselves and the English traders against attempts of the French who were then marching to attack them.*[82]

Trent's current house at that time, of course, was on the Virginia side of the North Branch of the Potomac and the mouth of Will's Creek. The Potomac River served as a boundary between the colony of Maryland and land where Trent's house resided, in Frederick County, Virginia.[83]

The Virginia side acreage owned by Lord Thomas Fairfax was purchased on January 29, 1750, by Thomas Cresap and Hugh Parker[84] to have the most convenient place to begin the Ohio Company trade.

Using the former Fairfax property as the site of the "new" Ohio Company warehouse or factory, the lots and few surrounding trading houses along with it became known as the "New Store Tract." The New Store was where the men of William Trent would depart on January 5 for the mouth of Redstone Creek and was where a young Major George Washington came to Christopher Gist's house to accompany him north to Fort Le Boeuf on November 14, 1753.

Some of these houses where traders such as William Trent and his wife, Sarah,[85] resided ranged from forty-five by twenty-five feet to forty-four by twenty feet.[86] They were two stories high, could fit up to a family of five, had good airy cellars for storing skins and, of course, had a counting room for expenses transacted. It was also known that anyone renting such houses from the Ohio Company would also be given two good bateaux for use.[87]

Now, as previously mentioned, the artificers sent out by Ohio Company factor William Trent were assumed by Washington to be heading to build a fort at the Forks, but where were they actually headed? A fort built at the Forks of the Ohio was the Ohio Company's ultimate goal, but no official orders had been given to Trent yet. In fact, the day Trent left his house with

Present-day site of the Ohio Company's "New Store Tract" and now currently the town of Ridgeley, West Virginia. *Courtesy of the author.*

supplies was also ironically the day the Governor's Council had discussed giving Trent a commission.[88] So, as it turned out, the Forks of the Ohio *was* their intended destination, but Trent wanted to get a jumpstart on things and first sent them to begin building a storehouse at the mouth of Redstone Creek.[89] Located seventy miles from the Inhabitants, the mouth of Redstone Creek emptied itself directly into the Monongahela River.

It was no secret that the Inhabitants was a considerable distance for transporting supplies to an outpost at the Forks, so being only thirty-seven miles from the mouth of the Monongahela, this storehouse could now be the first convenient place for laying stores to be transported by water.

Most of these "stores" came with Trent as he left the New Store. Unfortunately, with the rough trail through the mountains in January and traveling with fourteen horses[90] loaded with supplies, Trent took nine days to travel to the mouth of Redstone Creek. He would arrive there on January 30, 1754,[91] wasting no time in stating that "he immediately sent a messenger to acquaint the Indians that I had brought them some arms, and ammunition and to meet me at the mouth of the Monongahela that I might deliver them."[92] Bribery, it seemed, was to get full support of the Six Nations to begin a fort at the Forks of the Ohio.

View of the Monongahela River from the mouth of Redstone Creek in Brownsville, Pennsylvania. *Courtesy of the author.*

Word also reached Trent's former business partner George Croghan (pronounced "crow-han"),[93] who was conducting business at Logstown and his trading house at Pine Creek, because he made mention of Trent's arrival at Redstone in a letter on February 3, 1754, to Governor Hamilton of Pennsylvania:

> *Mr. Trent is just Come outt with ye Virginia goods and has brought a quantity of toules and workmen to begin a fort, and as he Can't talk the Indian languidge, I am obliged to stay and assist him in delivering them goods, which is Mr. Montour's advice.*[94]

After much debate over the years among historians, it does not appear that Trent and Croghan were in-laws. There is no primary evidence showing that they were related. Neither of their last wills written in 1782 and 1784,[95] respectively, left evidence of it, nor do any correspondence between them refer to each other as relation by marriage.

We can only speculate how much Trent spoke of the native language, for in the same letter he also verbally accosted trader John Davidson,[96] saying that "one John Davison, who talks a little of ye Indian language," even

Above: View of the site of George Croghan's trading house at the mouth of Pine Creek, now in Etna, Pennsylvania. *Courtesy of the author.*

Left: Historical marker of Logstown along Duss Avenue in Baden, Pennsylvania. *Courtesy of the author.*

though Davidson was the Indian interpreter George Washington personally chose among those residing at Logstown to convene with the Half King as they journeyed north to see the French outposts in 1753.

Although much is unknown regarding Croghan's early life, there is little doubt as to his earliest known trade with the Indians. This small account found tucked away in Trent's Remarks in 1757 gives hindsight as to his earliest known whereabouts, which had recently been inconclusive at best. Trent had written that Croghan told him firsthand: "In the year 1739, 1740, 1741, 1742, 1743, I traded at Giahaga,[97] a small creek which empties itself into Lake Erie on which Creek was three Indian Towns settled by the Six Nations, Wyandots, and Ottawas."[98]

Further proof appeared at the bottom of the account, where Trent added, "Mr Croghan gives this Accot." It was while trading around Lake Erie that Croghan would gain knowledge of the Indian languages, so whatever his motivation was currently and whether just fueled by being envious of his rival traders, this problem between the traders treaded lightly behind the task at hand at Redstone.

This storehouse was made of logs with loopholes,[99] and its dimensions were estimated as thirty feet long by twenty-two feet wide.[100] This was also the same Ohio Company building that the French would call "Le Hangard"[101] and would be left in ashes two days later after the Battle of the Great Meadows on July 6, 1754.[102] Further proof of this is found in the Remarks, where Trent not only wrote, "Monsieur De Villiers[103] likewise acknowledges the burning of the Hangard the Ohio Company Storehouse" but also mentioned something interesting about the Battle of Fort Necessity never seen until now.

Trent mentioned that the Indians told him "the French allowed their Indians to raise Lt. Mercier of the King's Troops after he was buried and scalp him without interfering in the least." (See Appendix VIII.)

Lieutenant Peter Mercier was the second in command under Captain James MacKay[104] of the South Carolina Independent Company, and although it was already known that he was killed at the Great Meadows, this is the first account of any soldier, let alone an officer, being buried at the Great Meadows. Even as this book is being written, no bodies have ever been found on the site of Fort Necessity National Battlefield.[105] It could be assumed that since Lieutenant Mercier was a high-ranking officer, Washington and MacKay had him buried to prevent such desecration, hoping he wouldn't be robbed or scalped, but that wasn't the case here. Washington would learn from this experience, it seemed, as almost a year later to the day, on July 13,

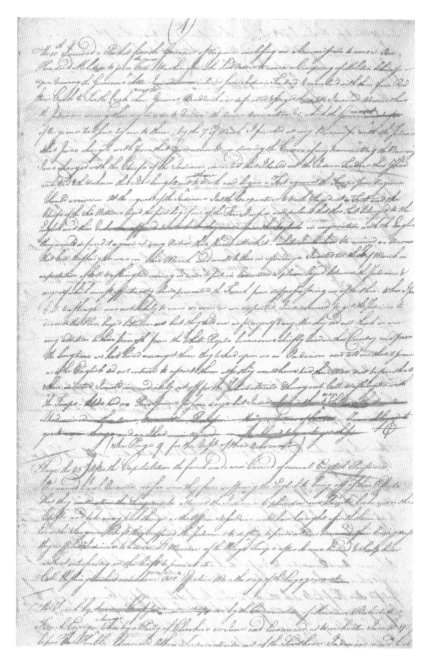

Page four of "Trent's Remarks," circa summer of 1757, mentioning the commission of William Trent and the burial of Lieutenant Peter Mercier of the Carolina Independents or "King's Troops" in 1754. *Courtesy of the William L. Clements Library at the University of Michigan in Ann Arbor, Michigan.*

1755, when he ordered to bury his superior, General Edward Braddock,[106] in the road just two miles from the Great Meadows after disastrous defeat eight miles from Fort Duquesne.

Fortunately, on February 10, 1754,[107] Trent was only at the storehouse at Redstone Creek a little over a week when Thomas Cresap arrived carrying an express from Williamsburg. In it were a packet of papers from Governor Dinwiddie and the news for which he had been waiting. Trent was not only commissioned a captain, but he also now had official orders to march to the Forks and help with building of a fort there.

After paying Cresap four pounds[108] for delivering it, Trent realized that he had further evidence these were orders for an Ohio Company fort. There was no money or letters of credit sent by the Virginia government, so he would do the only thing a factor would do. Trent would pay the raised men of his company with Ohio Company funds. After all, these men were the first raised troops and volunteers for Virginia.

Chapter 4

ORDERS GIVEN BY DINWIDDIE

T he official date of William Trent's commission he received at the mouth of Redstone Creek was January 26, 1754 (see Appendix II). It came one day after George Washington was commissioned and ordered to raise one hundred men from Augusta and Frederick Counties.[109] Despite being commissioned as a lieutenant colonel, Washington was instructed by Dinwiddie to "act on the defensive"[110] and "use all Expedition in proceeding to the Forks of the Ohio with the men under Com'd and there you are to finish and compleat in the best manner and as soon as You possibly can, the Fort w'ch I expect is there already begun by the Ohio Comp'a."[111]

Trent's initial orders were quite different and somewhat explicit. It could be because Trent was more experienced. Although he was never a military adjutant of two different proprieties like Washington, he had seen more military action than he when he successfully drove off the ambuscade of two hundred French and Indians on April 7, 1747.[112] In fact, that year Trent was also directly commissioned by the king despite joining in Philadelphia, an honor that thankfully Washington never would achieve. More impressively, Trent was a major landowner in several regions, successfully holding the title of justice of the peace as a gentleman in Cumberland County, Pennsylvania, and Frederick County, Virginia, where he then resided.[113] Trent also had experience in manual exercise having served as one of the four captains of the Pennsylvania-raised Independent Companies in 1746 and as ordered by Governor Thomas "to be diligent in teaching facings, Wheeling and Firings that they may Load and Fire quick and regular."[114]

This could be the reason why Dinwiddie ordered Trent to "keep possession of His M'y Lands on the Ohio and the Waters thereof and to dislodge and drive away and in case of refusal and resistance to kill and destroy or take Prisoners all and every Person and Persons not Subjects of the King of G.B."[115]

Surprisingly, that statement did not suggest defensive actions be taken, nor did his instructions in the packet of papers, which mentioned, "As You have a good Interest with the Ind's I doubt not You will prevail with many of them to join you in order to defeat the Designs of the French in taking their lands from them by Force of Arms."[116] With these orders quite clear and with little time to execute them in, Trent spared no time.

Luckily, there was more than one account of what happened next. In addition to the Trent's Remarks of 1757, there are also two separate accounts given on May 7, 1754,[117] and June 30, 1756,[118] by the eventual ensign of Trent's company, Edward Ward. Ward, who had previously worked as a clerk with Croghan and Trent at their tanning yard along the Conodoguinet Creek in 1750, said that "after Trent received the Governor's Instructions, he dispatched messengers to several parts of the country,"[119] a task Trent himself admitted was necessary "since there was no house nigh than two miles or inhabitants closer than twenty miles."[120]

According to Ward, it was one of these messengers who arrived and told him about Trent receiving such instructions at the place he resided.[121] Although it isn't clear where Edward Ward was living at the time, he did mention that after "Trent got Rafts made and every other thing necessary for his march[122]…Captain Trent marched from Redstone Creek to the mouth of the Monongahela where a number of Indians met him at which time and place this Deponent was present having met Captain Trent on his march." Ward had met Trent somewhere between Redstone Creek and the Forks, so one can only assume that they met along the Sewickley Old Town Path[123] while Ward was at Swiegly Old Town,[124] a place at the mouth of Sewickley Creek twenty-five miles from the Forks and where coincidentally his half brother, George Croghan, had a current plantation with grain in the ground.[125] This particular tract at Sewickley Creek Croghan had purchased earlier from the Half King and Scarouady[126] at Logstown in August 1749.[127]

What Ward failed to mention in detail was that Trent and his newly raised men made one stop before they eventually arrived at the Forks. In Trent's Remarks of 1757, Trent noted:

I had then some Carpenters with me and had a strong fortified Store House built at the Mouth of Redstone Creek, it being the first convenient place for laying stores be transported by Water to the Mouth of Monongahela, when the Ohio Company had given me orders to have a Fort built. The 10th I received a Packet from the Governor of Virginia enclosing me a Commission to raise one Hundred Militia to join the now Colonel Washington who had orders to raise a company likewise-Upon receiving the Governor's letter, I enlisted some Indian Traders. I marched with them from Redstone Creek to Turtle Creek near to where General Braddock was defeated and stayed there till I received advice that the Indians were gathering in orders to receive the Arms, Ammunition, which the Government of Virginia had sent by me to them.[128]

Turtle Creek was the newfound residence of trader and gunsmith John Fraser, who after twelve years living at Venango on the west side of the Allegheny River and the mouth of French Creek[129] was suggested by Washington to "provide large Qu'ty of Venison, Bear &c."[130] Fraser would be not only a neighboring asset for food but also Trent's second in command and a "suitable lieutenant to co-operate with him."[131]

Present-day site of Swiegly Old Town at the mouth of Sewickley Creek in West Newton, Pennsylvania. *Courtesy of the author.*

46

Fraser had one stipulation, however: that he would remain at his cabin at Turtle Creek for his pressing business and not be present at the site of the Forks unless required to do so. This eventually would become an issue in the coming months.

The temporary delay at Turtle Creek only lasted a few days. The gathering of the Six Nations would rely on one person, and Trent knew whose words mattered the most—and it wasn't Governor Dinwiddie's. It was the Half King, and he stayed with John Fraser until he heard word from him.

Silver shilling with an image of a young King George II, dated 1739. *Courtesy of Missouri History Museum.*

On a positive note, it gave Trent more time to recruit for his company. He was supposed to raise one hundred men in Augusta County and exterior settlements in the Dominion,[132] but to rapidly increase his men to meet that adequate number, he would have to repeat what he did raising men in Philadelphia back in June 1746. The key for Trent was that he didn't need the best soldiers—he just needed the right men. Of course, it didn't hurt either that compensation for the first raised volunteers[133] in Virginia was still two shillings a day. As to what kind of men he needed, Trent had developed a past reputation for enlisting criminals and runaway servants,[134] but mostly he recruited traders who knew every path to and from the Forks. This included former Ohio Company employees and those trader helpers and backwoodsman who resided in the most perilous areas of the upper and lower Ohio Country.

It is very doubtful the men of William Trent or Trent himself were uniformed. Months after these men were already at the Forks on March 28, 1754, Dinwiddie suggested to Maryland governor Horatio Sharpe[135] about purchasing a red uniform for the Virginia Regiment being raised by Washington and Fry "in order to have them in an Uniform, they allow a deduct'n from their Pay to purchase a Coat and Breeches of red Cloth."[136] There was, however, one item of clothing purchased by Trent from the Ohio Company one month before he left for Redstone. Trent had purchased from the warehouse three yards of cambrick[137] on December 10, 1753. Trent's men also carried their own personal weapons and accoutrements, for Dinwiddie even assumed, "I doubt not the Woodsmen You may enlist will be provided with Guns &c."[138]

View of the present-day site of John Fraser's cabin at the mouth of Turtle Creek from Westinghouse Bridge in North Versailles, Pennsylvania. *Courtesy of the author.*

The good news was that if the men of Trent's Company had weapons in need of repair, or did not carry one, Dinwiddie had commissioned John Carlyle of Alexandria, Virginia, as commissary of stores and provisions on January 26, 1754.[139] Dinwiddie wrote to Trent suggesting that Carlyle "will supply You accordingly with what Necessaries You may want and in case of want of Guns I have sent some to his care to be delivered to the Com'd'rs of either of these Comp'a giving receipt accordingly for them."[140]

Dinwiddie also had final instructions before he went before the House of Burgesses that he related on February 14: "When You have completed Y'r Comp'a send me a List thereof and the time of their enlisting and the Places of the of their Abroad." It wasn't until February 17, 1754, that Trent received word from the chiefs of the Six Nations. The time had finally come, and Trent took his fourteen horses loaded with presents from Dinwiddie and ensign Edward Ward and headed the eight miles to the Forks of the Ohio.

Chapter 5

TRUSTING ONE MAN

As Trent was set to arrive at the Forks, Dinwiddie addressed the House of Burgesses with haste and concern. He knew that the two hundred men under Washington and Trent he ordered to protect the fort builders would not be sufficient—not if what Washington claimed in his report was true after returning from the French outposts. Washington informed Dinwiddie that

> they were then preparing all Necessaries for building another Fort on that River, that they had 220 Canoes made, and many more hew'd to be made in order to transport early this spring, a great Number of regular Forces, not less than 1500 men, with their Ind's in F'dship with them, down the River Ohio, in order to build many more Fortress on it and that they propos'd Logstown to be the chief Place of their rendezvous.[141]

He had to act fast but also had to persuade the House of Burgesses once again that he had no ulterior motives other than those pertaining to the Crown of Great Britain. There had been suspicions ever since he arrived in the colonies around November 21, 1751,[142] on the same ship that carried Ohio Company cargo for George Mason.[143] Merely coincidental, it was nonetheless no secret that Dinwiddie held the Ohio Company in high esteem since he was a prominent member before he left England.[144]

In recent months, though, it was Dinwiddie's enforcement of the pistole fee[145] on patented lands in Virginia that made the burgesses question his motives once again. His response on November 28, 1753, to the burgesses would have been just as meaningful in February:

The Welfare and Happiness of Virg'a I have very much at Heart, and this great Point has been the chief Object of my Attention ever since I had the Hon'r to preside over this Dom'n, and have been influenc'd by no Other Motive and my Conduct upon all and extraordinary Occasions have been regulated by the Advice of the Council.[146]

Dinwiddie then explained to the burgesses about the "inconsistencies with the Treaties subsisting between the two Crowns"[147] and, as he called it, the "insults on our Sovereign's Protection and Barbarities on our Fellow Subjects."[148] Knowing that the burgesses would resent the recent threats to His Majesty's land, he made sure he suggested that "you will enable me by a full and sufficient Supply to exert the most vigorous Efforts to secure the rights and assert the Honour and Dignity of our Sovereign; to drive away those cruel and treacherous Invaders of your Properties."[149] And by his most vigorous efforts to secure the rights, Dinwiddie made sure to mention how he and his council had

arrayed some part of the Militia, w'ch I have order'd up to the Ohio, with all possible Expedition, to build a Fort there at the Forks of Monongahela, and as His M'y's gracious Present of 30 Pieces of Cannon, 80 lbs Powder and other Ordinance Store suitable one arriv'd, I have sent Ten of Cannon and a Proportion of Ammunition to Alexandria to be from thence as soon as possible to the Ohio.[150]

In truth, he hadn't sent all thirty cannons, as he was worried they would be too heavy to be carried on the march to the Ohio. Unfortunately, his assumptions were correct, and Washington would eventually leave them behind at Job Pearsall's house[151] for that very reason before even reaching Will's Creek.

Meanwhile, at the Forks of the Ohio, as Trent waited for more of the Six Nations to arrive and his men to meet them, he wrote to Washington to give the current situation at the Forks. Although the letter was written at Yaughyaughgany Big Bottom, which was also known as Swiegly Old Town, it was dated February 19, 1754. It stated that "the 17th Trent had arrived at the Forks of the Monongahela and met Mr. Gist and several others: In 2 or 3 days they expected down all the People and as soon as they came were to lay the Foundation of the Fort, expecting to make out for that Purpose about 70 or 80 men."[152] Coincidentally, just down the Ohio at Logstown, that number was assumed to be much larger, according to one Indian, Dejiquequé,[153] who told the French residing there on February 26 that "the English, numbering One Thousand men were to arrive in three days at the fork firstly to take possession of the aforesaid Monongahela River and that they were to call all the Nations from here to go meet this party."[154]

George Croghan was there—as it was known from his previously mentioned letter on February 3—but he may not have been the only one to join Trent from Logstown. In the Ohio Company records, fifty-two men joined them from February 15 to April 12, including trader and Washington's former interpreter John Davidson,[155] who eventually ventured down. As did Indian trader John Owens, who not only resided currently at Logstown but who had also helped Trent deliver the first set of presents[156] when Trent had been there in July to speak to the Half King.[157]

Ironically, though, the extract of Trent's letter was not the biggest headline in the Maryland and Virginia newspapers. On February 19, 1754, Governor Dinwiddie issued a proclamation

> *encouraging men to enlist in his Majesty's service for the Defense and Security of this Colony. And one Hundred Thousand Acres to be on or near contiguous to said Fort and another Hundred Thousand acres to be on or near River Ohio still be laid off and granted to such persons who by their voluntary engagement and Good Behaviour in the said Service shall desire the same.*[158]

Dinwiddie needed men, and this seemed the quickest way to get this to happen. Plus offering land grants for said service in the Ohio Country was almost too good for anyone looking for employment or reasonable money to resist.

Just to ensure this wasn't missed by anyone's eyes, Dinwiddie made certain that this announcement was "read and published at the Court Houses's, Churches and Chapels in each County within this Colony."[159] This would also assist Washington, who, if the reports around Williamsburg were true, was having trouble recruiting men for his company.

On the other hand, unlike Washington, Trent was not having problems enlisting volunteers. Ever since he headed toward the Forks and sent the word out, men had begun arriving since February 15.[160] He hadn't begun to lay out the fort yet, as he felt it was of greater importance to begin a treaty

Half King and Trent at the Forks, by Robert Griffing. *Courtesy of Paramount Press Inc.*

with the chiefs of the Six Nations and deliver the presents he had brought personally from Winchester.

Another reason for his haste with the presents was the status of the powder. Over 150 miles he had carried it in purple halfthick bags[161] through snow in the mountains and rain through the west of Laurel Hill to the Ohio, and he worried about damaging it. Usually, he used his own skin wrappers to prevent dampness, but realizing that he carried no matchcoat pieces of deerskin, Trent had to "buy two Pieces of Matchcoats for Inside Wrappers, one piece being the outside ones in the Bundles were damaged which I gave to the Indians."[162]

After carefully distributing the powder, lead and flints, he showed them the gift of wampum he brought. In one belt, he had three thousand black and three hundred white beads.[163] This combination of colors was meant to symbolize duality in the world—the sun and moon and the light and dark.[164] For the Six Nations, it meant that they and the English could be joined together at not only the Forks but also in the Ohio Country.

Ironically, this same wampum belt would be mentioned at a council held with several Indians and Pennsylvania governor Robert Hunter Morris in Philadelphia on December 19, 1754. Describing the events leading up to his account of the bloody skirmish in the bower with the French on May 28, 1754, Oneida chief Scarouady talked about the belt:

This belt was sent by the Governor of Virginia and delivered by Captain Trent. You see it in the representation of an hatchet. It was an invitation to us to join with and assist our brethren to repel the French from the Ohio. At the time it was given, there were but four or five of us, and we were all that knew any thing about the matter; when we got it, we put it into a private pocket on the inside of our garment. It lay next our breasts. As we were on the road going to Council with our brethren, a company of French, in number thirty-one, overtook us and desired us to go and council with them; and when we refused, they pulled us by the arm and almost stripped the chain of covenant from off it, but still I would suffer none to go with them. We thought to have got before them, but they passed us; and when we saw they endeavored to break the chain of friendship, I pulled this belt out of my pocket and looked at it and saw there this hatchet, and then went and told Colonel Washington of these thirty-one French Men, and we and few of our brothers fought with them. Ten were killed and twenty-one were taken alive whom we delivered to Colonel Washington, telling him that we had blooded the edge of his hatchet a little.[165]

Trent then personally gave presents to the most important voices of the Six Nations, the Half King and Scarouady. For each of them and their wives, he gave them a case of Neat[166] pistols and two ruffled shirts. He would declare them as a "particular present sent by the Governor himself to them."[167]

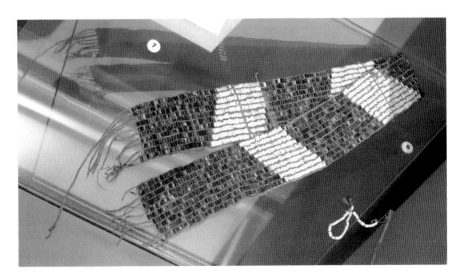

Black-and-white wampum belt of the Six Nations commemorating peace. *Courtesy of the author.*

Yet as the Indians accepted the gifts graciously, they all knew what they were really at this treaty for. Surprisingly, the chiefs of the Six Nations singled Trent out and told him exactly what they wanted for an outpost to be built at the Forks. It was described in Trent's own words as he explained what they told him in his remarks:

> *During the Course of my transacting the business I was charged with, the Chiefs of the Indians insisted that I should set the Indian traders that I had enlisted & the Workmen that I had brought out with me to work and begin a Fort against the Troops from Virginia should arrive.*[168]

They also made one last suggestion that Trent begin immediately. "At the request of the Indians," he wrote, "I set the Carpenters to work & layed out a fort."[169]

Trent began just above the high embankments at the Point,[170] walking with the Indians to clear and lay out the square first, possibly using the original plan[171] of the fort they were to build at Chartier's Creek back in July, which was still in the Ohio Company books and approximated at ninety feet on a side.

The suggested plan was "sawed or hewed loggs and to inclose a piece of Ground ninety foot square besides the Four Bastions of the Corners of sixteen feet square each with houses in the middle for Stores, Magazines."[172] Then Trent, along with help of a measuring wheel[173] and possibly a circumferentor,[174] would stake the corners and midpoints to preserve these dimensions.

These proposed buildings were to be made from the abundance of white and red oak timber[175] felled in the area while Trent had begun the treaty. Like the promise of protecting their families with the new fort at the Forks, Trent wisely allowed the Half King to preface the fort's new beginning by "laying the First log of one of the Storehouses."[176]

Trent's description of this account is also the first account to prove that more than one building was under construction at the Forks, as the logs were being sawed, hewed and crisscrossed onto his layout.

The Half King was quite honored to lay the first log; he declared at that very moment, "This fort belonged to the English and them, injunction with the English they would defend it against any nation that should attack it."[177]

Meanwhile, eighteen miles up the Ohio at Logstown, word was received about this very same assemblage of men at the Forks. On March 6, 1754, ensign Michel Chauvignerie[178] sent scouts to the mouth of the Monongahela to find out exactly what the English were building. According to their translated report on March 7, 1754:

> [T]*he scouts arrived at the village of the Loups,*[179] *having no hope of finding a carriage to cross the river. The scouts made to cross to an island opposite to the establishment where they took notice an advanced house almost made which is to serve as a Magazine, but because of the distance they could not know in what manner they were constructing their fort, since it was still only marked out.*[180]

One of the scouts was a deserter of the Illinois Country who noted, "[T] en leagues in the same river where they made a warehouse[181] where he said there are six cannons which must go to this house."[182]

According to the later accounts at the Forks, no mention is given to any pieces of cannons being present there with Trent or Ward. On April 4, 1754, George Washington even wrote to the governor of Pennsylvania, James Hamilton, stating that "when Mr. Ward Ensign to Capt. Trent's Company was compelled to surrender his small Fort in the Forks of Monongialo to the French, who having but an inconsiderable Number of Men and no Cannon to make a proper Defense."[183]

So, if no pieces of artillery were taken to the Forks, then it is quite possible they were stored and locked behind the jousts[184] of the storehouse at Redstone Creek for such a purpose like the French scouts had said.

Neither Trent nor Ward said anything of artillery in his own account, but in a later account in the Contrecoeur Papers called the "Deposition of the English Deserters on March 20, 1755," three Englishmen were noted as captured near the mouth of Redstone Creek, shedding some light on a theory of where the artillery could have been. When questioned as to their intentions by the French, André Maynard, one of the three Englishmen, said that "he had been the third to come and get arms and tools which had been hidden last year when the English evacuated their first fort on La Belle Rivière[185] which stuff belonged to sundry individuals who come on the Belle Rivière with Captain Trent."[186]

Assuming that most items inside the storehouse belonged to men of Trent's men and the Ohio Company, then it is quite possible those twenty carpenters hauled a few pieces from the New Store magazine when they left on January 5. They just would unfortunately never make it to the Forks to aid in their eventual protection from the French if this was true.

It wouldn't be until March 7, 1754,[187] that Trent would finish his business with Indians at the Forks, and yet one thing still evidently bothered him. He had gotten about seventy[188] men in the recent weeks to protect the workmen, but where was Washington and his proposed company? Trent wrote with haste to Washington and urged him to come to the Ohio. Now that the presents were distributed, there was unrest among the Indians, for they had stated repeatedly over the last few days that "they all wanted to know why the English did not intend to assist them."[189]

Trent anxiously waited for a reply, wishing to know the same thing.

Chapter 6

BORROWED TIME

I n Alexandria, Virginia, Colonel Washington was in trouble. He had only
enlisted a less than adequate force in the last month, and those who
did refused to serve until they were paid their advance fee. He wrote to
Dinwiddie on March 9, 1754, saying, "I have increas'd my number of Men
ab't 25 and we daily Experience the great necessity for cloathing the Men as
we find the generality of those who are to be enlisted, are of those loose, Idle
Persons that are quite destitute of House and Home."[190]

To make the situation worse, the men required clothing, stockings and
even shoes. Washington also wrote, "There is many of them without
Shoes, others want Stocking, some are without Shirts and not a few that
have Scarce a Coat, or Waistcoat, to their Backs."[191] This was just cause
for Washington's delay, but Trent couldn't wait any longer. He knew that
all those with him at the Forks were on borrowed time. So, he wrote to
Washington again to speed up his march to the Forks. This time it was
Dinwiddie who was quite alarmed, and he expressed his concern to
Washington on March 12, 1754:

> Y'r two letters of the 3rd and 7thg Curr't I rec'd and the enclos'd from
> Messrs. Trent and Cresap. I am surprised from their Letters that the French
> are so Early expected down the Ohio; w'ch I think make it necessary for
> You to march what Soldiers You have enlisted, immediately to the Ohio and
> escort some Waggons, with the necessary provisons.[192]

A piece of dent corn.
Courtesy of the author.

It was true that Trent lacked men in comparison to the proposed French forces to the north, who at this point in time had arrived at Fort Presque Isle by March 8. He needed Washington's men and provisions. Trent had brought bags of Indian meal and flour from the New Store,[193] but after the Indians exhausted most of it during the treaty, there wasn't much left of it to even barter for freshly killed meat, as hunting on the proclaimed Indian lands of the Ohio Country was out of the question and considered a bylaw condition to having their permission to build a fort. As this came as a surprise to no one, the Delaware Indians clearly took great advantage of this, as Ensign Ward described, saying, "They offered great prices for any kind of meat they could bring in, even seven shillings and sixpence for a Turkey."[194] Now, as the days grew hotter, they were reduced to purchasing Indian corn without salt from the Delaware Indians who resided near the Forks.

Indian corn—or maize, as it was so called by European settlers first arriving to the colonies—was not just the traditional multicolored ornamental corn that is hung on doors today. "Indian corn," especially in the northern frontier of the upper Ohio Country such as the Forks of the Ohio, was probably a type of cross between generalized flint corn[195] and dent corn.[196] This type of corn was planted in the spring, harvested in late September or early October and shelled and dried to preserve its purpose to last over the winter months until more could be planted again. Regarding this in Ward's and Trent's respective accounts, they corroborated each other, saying that "they had to purchase Indian corn without salt." They purchased bits of native flint corn, but with the absence of salt, the "Indian meal" that Ward referred to after the "parched" corn was mashed extensively would at best make rough porridge after mixing with water. In actuality, it was a rather sparse meal for those working throughout the warm days.

But not all hope was lost. Word came from Christopher Gist that Washington with his detachment of the Virginia Regiment was on the march.[197] In the meantime, Trent strategized: "I know the great advantage it would be for the Troops to be provided with Stores and to have timber ready to raise the Fort against the arrival of troops that they immediately have a place of defense."[198]

Trent knew that as each day passed, they were also another day closer to the French arriving. Each day, he heard reports that they would come down from Venango, and Gist had told him that "a Chickasaw Indian had seen a force of 400 French coming up the river from the Falls of the Ohio."[199] They had to be prepared, and contrary to Ward's later claim that they were "having no place of defense but a few Pallisades,"[200] Trent executed a plan having little hope Washington would be arriving in the next few days. He also made sure that he made this plan only between the Indians and himself. Men were coming and going from the Forks, and he didn't need to lose any more from his dwindling number. It was also a plan he had supported from the beginning, dating back almost a year ago, when he expressed his opinion on the French invading the Ohio Country to his former employer's son, William Logan, back on May 8, 1753, from the mouth of Pine Creek: "We are in hopes five or six hundred will come while we are here that we may have the pleasure of helping the Indians kill a few of them which would be some satisfaction."[201]

Despite the somber reports, the lack of provisions and the heat, the men still worked diligently on the fort. In his Remarks, Trent was even impressed by their efforts, complimenting the workmen:

> *I constantly attended the work from daylight in the Morning till Night as everyone worked and every one seemed to have the good of the Country at heart, there was an incredible deal of Work done in this time.*[202]

George Croghan, who had been at the Forks since he met Trent on February 17, also shared this sentiment. On March 23, 1754, he wrote to Governor Hamilton:

> *Mr. Trent had received a Commission from the Governor of Virginia and had enlisted about Seventy Men before I left Ohio. I left him and his Men at the Mouth of Monongialo building a Fort, which seemed to give the Indians great Pleasure and put them in high Spirits.*[203]

Croghan had also a good reason to be in high spirits. A few weeks earlier, on March 2, 1754, he had purchased a horse from a Lancaster County Indian trader named Daniel Hart. The horse was a brown gelding natural pacer named Woolabarger.[204] Croghan would later leave on Woolabarger from the Forks without witnessing Trent's execution of his plan. The only problem was the Indians did not wish to follow through with the plan until Washington and his detachment arrived. But according to Trent, they proposed another suggestion: "they insisted I would immediately set off for the Inhabitants and hurry out Colonel Washington with his Troops."[205]

Until the discovery of this manuscript and the recent process of this author's research, no accurate date was ever known of when Trent left the Forks. Among most authors who touch on this historical event, the presumed theory was that he left on April 8, 1754, as this was the date of the account William Trent made for Governor Dinwiddie of all his expenses to and from the Forks and thus the assumed day when he left there to replenish his provisions at Will's Creek. Fortunately, with newly confirmed evidence, we can discuss the date in question and provide the correct one. Mentioned twice by Trent in his Remarks, the given date he says he left his men at the Forks was March 17, 1754:[206]

> I waited til the 17th of March in expectation of Col. Washington coming in order to put in execution a plan layed between the Indians and myself which must have effectively have preventing the French from dispossessing us at the Ohio.… [Further into his remarks, he mentions that same day again and the current situation at his chain of command:] I left my Men the 17th of March with the command of my Ensign, as my Lieutenant had not then joined me.[207]

He also gave a status of the fort construction, describing in detail before he left for the Inhabitants: "This time I had finished the storehouse, ready upon the spot for raising another and a large quantity of timber."[208]

With all the pressing work in the past few days, the fort was definitively more than just "an advance building with upright stakes"[209] at the Point. This construction pleased Trent when he left, but because of securing provisions from Fraser's cabin for the men until his return, it took Trent until March 27 to travel the 130 miles to reach the Inhabitants.[210]

He had hoped to see Washington and his detachment encamped near the Potomac River, but that was not meant to be. In fact, according to Ensign Ward's deposition of 1756, "[W]hen Trent arrived at his house where Fort Cumberland now stands, there was no account from the Regiments nor any Detachments from it nor any provisions set up there."[211] In actuality, Trent received a letter dated March 19 from Washington saying it would still be seven or eight days before the wagons were ready.[212]

At the Forks, with the recent hot weather, not much work was being done on the fort. The men were tired, scarcely getting by on unsalted Indian corn and waiting with heightened anxiety as to the other troops' arrival.

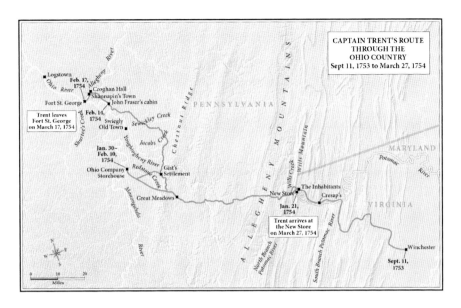

Captain Trent's route through the Ohio Country, September 11, 1753–March 27, 1754. *Courtesy of Glen Pawelski and Mapping Specialists Inc.*

It was soon after Trent left for the Inhabitants that Gist arrived at the fort and tried to remedy their lack of provisions. Taking with him several men suggested by Ward, Gist headed up the Monongahela to the mouth of Redstone Creek to gather more provisions from their new storehouse. (He would find out later that there were no provisions at Redstone and would not return until after hearing about the surrender at the Forks.)

Trent, on the other hand, gathered more provisions from the New Store and tried to recruit more volunteers to join him.[213] He didn't know that by April 4, the French had already been at Venango and were ready to disembark down the Allegheny. Back at the Forks, the last of Trent's men arrived on April 12.[214]

It was the next day when Ward received the news that he and his men had feared from the beginning: the French were coming in just four days. According to Ward, trader John Davidson had written to Robert Callender[215] and confirmed the truth "that they were to be down by that time." With four days left, they didn't have much time, so Ward quickly made some decisions. In his Remarks, Trent described one such decision, saying how "I understand nothing was done to fort after I left, except laying one log all around."[216]

It was the only known mention of Ward and the workmen laying logs horizontally around the marked fort, as if an extra defense was attempted before the French came down the river and the palisades were put up. The plan of defense would also be like the outpost built by James Burd[217] that had horizontal logs lying around the dwellings one mile north of Redstone Creek in 1759. Surprisingly, Ward also omitted this detail in both depositions in 1754 and 1756. He did decide to take Trent's advice in agreement with the Indians to lay out their plan of defense by making use of the large quantity of timber. The plan was to build a stockade around the almost completed two buildings where Trent marked in dimensions of the fort square.

Quickly, Ward cut the oak timber into palisades. Unfortunately, he wasn't sure what to do next, so after sending a copy of John Davidson's letter to Trent at the Inhabitants, he decided to pay a personal visit to his other superior, Lieutenant John Fraser, just eight miles up the Monongahela at Turtle Creek on April 14, 1754. As Ward described it, "It was late at night when he got there, Accompanied by Robert Roberts, Thomas Davison, Samuel Asdill[218] and an Indian and shew'd him the letter."[219]

But if Ward was looking for useful advice from Fraser, his somewhat jeering response took Ward by surprise. Fraser seemed to be unsympathetic to the account of French being only a few days from the Forks, saying to Ward that "he was well assured the French would be down, but said what we can do in the Affair."[220]

Ward was not giving up so easily. He sent for the Half King and Scarouady and told them to meet him at the Forks. Then he pleaded with Fraser again to uphold his duty as second in command and come down to the fort. Fraser, it seemed, had more pressing matters and refused, saying that "he had a shilling to loose for a Penny he should gain by his commission at that time and that he had business which he could not settle under Six Days with his Partner."[221]

Ward was frustrated but did not waste any more time and rode back down to the Forks, worried that the Indians of the Six Nations would leave if he didn't "hold out to the last Extremity."[222] He knew that the Delawares were already much inclined to the French, and he didn't want the other nations to follow if "it should be said that the English retreated like Cowards before the French Forces Appeared."[223]

Ward and the men continued to work on the palisades while keeping a cautious eye on the river. Trent's company numbered fewer than fifty men[224] now, and he hoped that they had a little more time before the French appeared or Trent and Washington arrived with more men and provisions.

On the night of April 16, almost three miles north of the Forks, the small Delaware Indian village of Shannopin's Town[225] became illuminated

View from the 31st Street Bridge of the present-day site of Shannopin's Town in the Strip District of Pittsburgh, Pennsylvania. *Courtesy of the author.*

with fires built by the French soldiers, who had arrived earlier in the day in pirogues[226] and bateaux.[227] The French commander who had once explored the Ohio Country with Céloron de Blainville in 1749[228] sat close near the fire, writing furiously with his quill. He signed his own name at the bottom, "Contrecoeur / Done at this camp April 16, 1754," and slowly he sealed the summons.[229] (See Appendix IX.)

The next day, April 17, was crucial, for the upcoming confrontation would form the opening sparks of what would be known later as the French and Indian War.

Chapter 7

ONE HOUR

On the night of April 16, three miles south at the Forks, Edward Ward had to be feeling frustrated and abandoned. Here he was the half brother of George Croghan, a resident of Cumberland County and East Pennsboro,[230] and he had no idea what the next day would bring. His captain and commander had not yet returned from the Inhabitants. His lieutenant refused to help at the Forks. There was no sign of Colonel Washington or his detachment, and worst of all, the only provisions left were bits of unsalted Indian corn.

Fortunately, the morning came without incident, but just after one o'clock in the afternoon, everyone, including Ward himself, saw them. Just two miles up from the fort, Ward said, "The French first appeared to him at Shannopin's Town the 17th of April last, that they moved down within a small distance from the Fort."[231]

The men stood inside their makeshift fort watching what the French did next through the palisades. The plan of defense was completed that morning, for Ward said that "they had the last Gate of the Stockade Fort erected before the French appeared to him."[232]

As to how many French appeared that day, the numbers are debatable. Ward first deposed on May 7, 1754, to Governor Dinwiddie that "he was credibly informed by an Englishman who attended the French Commandant that they had 300 wooden canoes and 60 battoes, and had four men to each Canoe and Battoe,[233] and they also had eighteen pieces of cannon, three of which were nine pounders."[234] The total number he

Present-day site of the French landing at the Forks of the Ohio on the afternoon of April 17, 1754, now currently Point State Park in Pittsburgh, Pennsylvania. *Courtesy of the author.*

described seeing that day was just under one thousand French and Indians who traveled with them.

Compare that now to his deposition of 1756, which provided more details but was only deposed to the Majesty's justice of Cumberland County, Samuel Smith.[235] In this account, Ward said that "there were the French Eleven hundred in number and that he saw several pieces of Cannon pointed at the Fort within musket shot but could not tell the number, but was afterwards told by the Indians there [were] nine pieces of Cannon."[236]

That's almost a difference of one hundred men and nine cannons. So why did Ward say there were fewer cannons and more French almost two years later? Assumptions can be drawn that he purposely exaggerated the French numbers and artillery to warrant sympathy from the governor for why they were forced to vacate their fort that very day.

There is, however, another account from Trent in his Remarks that also refers to an estimated number of French that day at the Forks:

As many believed that there was a good fort there and that I had delivered it up, tho I was not within a hundred Miles of the Place at the time, As well as the world knew what kind of place it was and what force was there at the time and the French army coming with 700 men and 9 pieces of Cannon (the same cannon which is at the time at Fort Duquesne) to attack my people there under the Command of Mr. Ward.[237]

Although this is a seemingly secondhand account since Trent heard about this later at the New Store, one can only wonder if Ward exaggerated the numbers out of being panic stricken at seeing so many at one time or if he just embellished the official report purposely to the governor—more than one thousand sounds a lot more serious than vacating the Forks so easily to merely half that number. Either way, the French soldiers they saw only humbled their adequate numbers while they clutched their guns inside the palisades and watched intently as the French disembarked from their canoes and bateaux.

There is no controversy about the numbers of Trent's company that day. Both Trent and Ward did agree it was "not quite fifty men including with the soldiers, the workmen and travelers that happened to be there at the time."[238] Ward specifically deposed before the governor a relatively similar number, saying, "That he then observeing the number of the French, which he judg'd to be about a Thousand and considering his own weakness being but Forty one in all, whereof only Thirty three were soldiers."[239]

So, outnumbered almost twenty to one and supposedly with cannons pointed at their small area of defense, what happened next could have altered everything. Ward said:

[T]*hey marched their men in a regular manner a little better than Gunshot of the Fort and that Le Mercier*[240] *a French officer sent by Contrecoeur the Commandant in Chief of the French Troops came with an Indian Interpreter called by the Mingoes*[241] *the Owl*[242] *and two Drums.*[243]

Le Mercier then presumably waved a red cloth on the tip of his sword to signal Ward that he wished to parley[244] and handed him the summons Contrecoeur had written the night before. Unfortunately, time was not again on their side. In fact, Le Mercier wanted a resolve almost immediately. Ward said, "Le Mercier presently deliver'd him the summons by the Interpreter, looked at his watch, which was about two, and gave him an hour to fix a resolution."[245]

Arrival of the French, by Pittsburgh native Nat Youngblood, 1969. *Courtesy of Robert MacLachlan.*

As if the pressure wasn't enough for Ward, he had only until 3:00 p.m. to review and respond to their terms. As he sat reviewing the summons, the Half King became his acting advisor in the matter at hand; he, too, was strategizing after Ward described how "the Half King received a belt of wampum, much to the same purpose."[246]

Thirty minutes would pass before any ideas came about, but the Half King suggested a tactic to bide Ward more time, or at least make his men's survival more likely. After all, he heard what happened in January 1753 to those recent traders like John Finley and others,[247] who were employed by the Ohio Company when they encountered the French.

Fortunately, the Half King's plan might have saved them both. "He advised to acquaint the French he was no Officer of rank or invested with powers to answer their Demands and requested them to Wait the Arrival of the principal Commander."[248] Waiting a day or two might be enough time for Trent or Washington to arrive at the Forks.

As the time reached three o'clock, Ward went accompanied by three men to the French camp. He took the Half King since he was his main advisor. Then he chose Rob't Roberts, a private soldier and former trader of George Croghan who had survived and lost his Ohio Company goods when the French and Indians burned Pickawillany in 1752. Lastly, he took John Davidson as an Indian interpreter so that the Half King could understand every word Ward spoke at the French camp.[249]

Contrecoeur, the French commandant, was not amused by the suggested advice or fooled by the delay tactic Ward tried to use. He demanded Ward give him an answer, saying that "he should not wait for an Answer from any other person, And absolutely insisted on his determining what to do that Instant, or he should immediately take Possession of the Fort by force."[250]

GOVERNOR
DUQUESNE

Portrait of French governor general of New France Michel-Ange Duquesne de Menneville. *Courtesy of the author.*

Ward looked at his men inside the fort and the hundreds of birch-bark canoes crowding the riverbank. He had no choice. He saw the artillery pointed at the fort and realized that he had to surrender the outpost. He did request Contrecoeur "to have them march off with everything belonging thereto by Twelve o'clock the next day,"[251] and the French commandant obliged, but with one stipulation: Contrecoeur wished Ward and his men to join the party of the Six Nations and encamp a rather considerable distance from the fort.[252]

Maybe it made the French commander less nervous knowing the Half King was farther away, or maybe it was so that there would be no extra ears listening when he invited the young ensign to dine with him.

Without hesitation, Ward graciously accepted his supper invitation, but faced with a barrage of questions concerning the English government, he wisely "told him he could give no Answer to, being unacquainted with such affairs."[253] He also declined Contrecoeur's repeated attempts to purchase his carpentry tools, politely saying that "he loved his King and Country too well to part with any of them."[254]

The French, despite evicting Ward and the rest of Trent's men from the Forks, did admire the early stages of their fort. It was evident when Contrecoeur wished to buy their tools, but even more so later in a letter dated May 11, 1754, when Governor Duquesne[255] said, "I am glad that you found a good supply of posts and squared timber; For the English are good judges of wood and excel in workmanship."[256] Evidently with such admiration for their handiwork, the two buildings built when Trent was there possibly were kept intact when the French built Fort Duquesne.

What the French did not keep standing, however, were the palisades Ward and his men had struggled to cut and hastily surround the marked square of the fort right before the French appeared on the river. The palisade removal would be the first order of business the next morning of the eighteenth, as Ward, toting a speech from the Half King, watched in the distance as they rounded up what little horses they could find. Sadly, that morning John Faulkner[257] and other hands of Captain Trent had already lost thirty-one horses and mares[258] from their possession and watched them roam freely close to the French camp. Ward knew that it would be best to leave them behind with the French, knowing full well how long it would be heading back up the Monongahela thirty-seven miles to the mouth of Redstone Creek. Before they left, though, Ward made sure that Washington received the bad news immediately. So, he sent itinerant James Foley to ride ahead as swiftly as he could and deliver the report to Washington.[259]

There was one individual that day, however, who did not travel with Trent's company and chose to stay behind to speak to the French. As the French tore out the palisades, the Half King became irate and infuriated. After all, he and Trent had laid out the plan of defense and the outline of the fort back in March, but like he told the French, "it was he who Order'd that fort and laid the first log of it himself."[260] To make matters worse, Ward

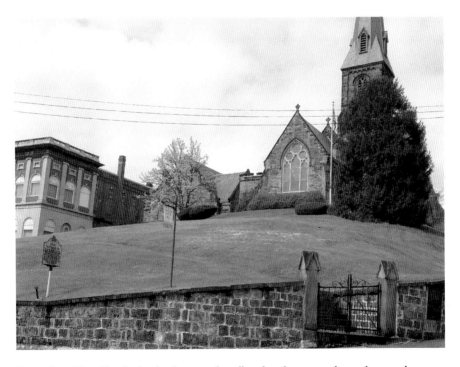

Exact site of Fort Cumberland, whose north wall and perimeter are located currently beneath Emmanuel Episcopal Church in Cumberland, Maryland—also called the Inhabitants before the fort was enlarged in 1755. *Courtesy of the author.*

said that even after "the Half King stormed greatly at the French, they paid no regard to what he said."[261]

In an account dated November 5, 1754, at Will's Creek, found in the National Archives of the United Kingdom,[262] we can hear and start to picture what happened next with the effect of the Half King's rage. The author of this account, an unidentified Ohio Iroquois warrior, told Colonel James Innes[263] through interpreter William Trent that

> *we were all with Capt. Trent's people when the French came down the Ohio and the Half King told the French they had no Business there on their hunting grounds pushing the French officer with his Hand, telling them he would not allow his Brother the English to be routed from the Land, which the half King by the Director's of the Six Nations had allowed them to build and fortify; upon which ensued a Scuffle and had there been any proper person with a small Body to have encouraged the Indians, they would not have left one Frenchman alive upon the Spot.*[264]

From what is described in detail, it seems that the situation was more intense on April 18 than when Le Mercier delivered the summons to Ward the day before. Fortunately, nothing materialized from it, but this did not change the fact that tensions were rising in the Ohio Country. As for the enraged Half King, his day in infamy would be coming sooner rather than later.

Chapter 8

THE SITUATION WORSENS
FOR TRENT

It took two days for Ward and his men to arrive back at the mouth of Redstone Creek. Although unmolested by the Indians, the remaining men of Trent's company had been watched and followed ever since they left the Forks.

One such eyewitness to Ward's departure was a man named Benjamin Kuykendall. Kuykendall lived on Peter's Creek[265] and would later be elected with Edward Ward as a gentleman justice[266] of Yohogania County in 1779. Yohogania County was one of three counties joining Monongalia and Ohio Counties that was formed from the District of West Augusta in 1776. Yohogania's county seat was on the Monongahela (where present-day Jefferson Hills lies) and very near Benjamin Kuykendall's place of residence.

It was also Kuykendall who said on October 26, 1779, in the minutes of the Courts of Yohogania County that

> *in the Spring of the year 1754, he saw Major Edward Ward on his march to Virginia from what is now Fort Pitt. Major Ward had command of the party with him and understood that he was the commanding officer of the post at the aforesaid place as an officer in the Virginia line and surrendered to the French.*[267]

This also gave further proof that the men of William Trent followed the same route as they did in February, when they arrived back at the storehouse at Redstone Creek on April 20. Ironically, this route along the Sewickley

The grave of Benjamin Kuykendall (1722–1789) at Peters Creek Cemetery in Clairton, Pennsylvania. *Courtesy of the author.*

Old Town path through Turtle Creek would also be part of the road Trent would suggest to James Burd on September 29, 1758,[268] to gain access to Fort Duquesne from Bouquet's breastworks eight miles away.[269]

Meanwhile, on April 19, Washington, waiting for his detachment at Job Pearsall's, received an express from the Inhabitants from William Trent. The letter was of concern since Trent expressed his words with urgency. Washington said that "he demanded a Reinforcement with all Speed as he hourly expected a Body of Eight Hundred French."[270]

To Washington, this was sooner than expected. So, he wrote to Colonel Joshua Fry[271] to alert him of the pending French arrival at the Forks and then rode with his detachment to Colonel Cresap's at Shawnee Old Town. A few days later, he received the first unfortunate report confirmed in person by the interim commander at the Forks himself, Edward Ward, who declared firsthand

> *that he an ensign of Captain Trent had been obliged to surrender to a body of one thousand French and upwards, under the command of Captain Contrecoeur who was from Venango with Sixty Battoes and Three hundred canoes, and who having planted eighteen pieces of cannon against the Fort afterwards had sent him a Summons to depart.[272]*

There was still some silver lining, according to Washington, because before Ward handed him the speech from the Half King, "he informed him the Indians were still attached to our Interest."[273] So not all was lost, especially since two Mingoes traveled with Ward from the Forks so they could see for themselves the troops marching alongside them.

Despite the slight ray of hope, the troubling news of the surrender at the Forks still left Washington in a quandary. Should he advance closer to the Forks or should he await further orders from Governor Dinwiddie and Colonel Fry?

On April 23, 1754, Washington held a council of war to discuss the summons from Contrecoeur and whether the 150 men in his detachment were sufficient once they combined with Trent's men, whom Ward sadly informed Washington were reduced to only 33 effective men.

This was not the time to be foolish, and according to Washington, "It was thought a Thing impracticable to march towards the Fort without sufficient Strength."[274] The council did decide, however, that it would be agreeable to march as far as the Ohio Company storehouse at Redstone Creek, clearing a road so that the artillery and baggage could pass through. They all resolved this motion based on three reasons:

> *1st, That the Mouth of Red-Stone Creek is the first convenient Place on the River Monaungahela. 2d, That Stores are already built at that Place for the provisions of the Company, wherein our Ammunition may be laid up, our great Guns may be also sent by Water whenever we should think it convenient to attack the Fort. 3d, We may easily (having all the Conveniences) preserve our People from the ill Consequences of Inaction,*

and encourage the Indians our Allies to remain in our Interest. Whereupon, I sent Mr. Wart to the Governor, with one of the young Indians and an Interpreter, I thought it proper also to acquaint the Governors of Maryland and Pennsylvania of the News.[275]

There was only one problem with the initial plan though: Trent's men still hadn't arrived yet from the Ohio. After storing sundry items at the storehouse at Redstone Creek, they had slowly made their way back at their own leisure, not caring in the least about Ward's urgency to ride ahead and confirm the bad news immediately to Washington.

In fact, four of them (who initially worked for the Lowrey brothers) stayed behind and, instead of following the others, traveled east to where the path forked and set up shop at Gist plantation to sell their goods. Coincidentally, they began to trade with two well-known French Indians, English John and the Owl, who had followed them since they left the Forks. The Owl, of course, was Le Mercier's interpreter when he initially handed the summons to Ward just less than a week earlier.

Now, what happened next is unclear, but amid the dealings, a somewhat violent altercation occurred and ended with three of them—Nehemiah Stevens, Elizabeth Williams[276] and Andrew McBriar[277]—being captured and sent to Fort Duquesne. The fourth in their party, John Kennedy, who was wounded in the dispute, was later taken to the fort like the others, where he eventually recovered.[278]

It would be two more days before Trent's men would finally arrive at the Inhabitants. On April 25, they rolled into Washington's encampment. To say they were ill tempered was an understatement. They became so troublesome that Washington later admitted in his letter to Dinwiddie that "Capt Trent's men who by their refractory behavior did oblige me to separate them from the other Soldiers."[279]

Trent's men, tired and irritable from their journey from the Forks, were ordered to go across the river and remain at the New Store until further orders were given. Unfortunately, this only made them

Historical marker of Gist Plantation, located along Route 119 in Mount Braddock, Pennsylvania. *Courtesy of the author.*

angrier. Frustrated with an unreliable Washington, they defied his orders to remain a part of his detachment and dispersed on their own accord.[280]

The truth came to light about the real motivation behind dispersing independently, however. According to Washington, "The men belonging to Captain Trent, who by your orders have been inlisted as Militia-Troops, the Officers having imprudently promised them Two shillings per Day, they now refuse to serve for less Pay."[281] Yet who could blame them? Why serve for eight pence, the standard soldier's daily rate, when they were paid three times[282] that by William Trent?

Washington, thankful to rid himself of these men retarding his advance, didn't actually lose all of Trent's men. There were three, according to the author's current research, who stayed and reenlisted in the Virginia Regiment. There was Samuel Arsdale, the Irish trader who stood five-foot-seven from Frederick County, Virginia.[283] Edward Lucas was another, an Indian trader and one of the earliest settlers of Frederick County.[284] The third, named Jacob Arrants, was also an Indian trader, but unlike the others, he was acknowledged specifically by Washington because "he was Master of the Indian language and perfectly acquainted with all the way and mountains between this and ye Fork."[285]

Edward Ward would also be of special service because he was ordered to deliver his report of what happened at the Forks to Governor Dinwiddie in Williamsburg. Ward would buy Washington's horse and saddle[286] and arrive at the governor's residence on May 4, 1754. His deposition, though somewhat bold and descriptive, unfortunately did not provide the most positive light for his superiors, William Trent and John Fraser.

Almost immediately, Dinwiddie was obviously displeased with Ward's initial report and expressed his frustration as he wrote directly to the commander of the Virginia Regiment, Colonel Joshua Fry:

> *I am advised Capt. Trent and his Lieut. Fraser have been long absent from their duty, leaving Ensign Ward with ab't 23 men only, to guard the workmen while preparing Materials to erect the Fort begun and (who was) oblig'd to surrender on the Sumons of the French Com'd'r; Which Conduct and Behavior I require and expect You will enquire into at a Court Martial, and give Sentence accordingly.[287]*

Dinwiddie also wrote to Washington on May 4 but was a little more direct as to his feelings toward Trent and Fraser, in the final part of that letter saying:

*The ill conduct of Capt. Trent and L't. Fraser in leav'g the Fort witho't
Leave, meets with just resentm't here. I have order'd Colo. Fry to try them
by a Court Martial w'n I hope, they will meet with such Punishment as
this unaccountable Action deserves.*[288]

There is no evidence existing that a court-martial ever took place for
Trent or Fraser. No firsthand accounts were found relating to the notion
by Dinwiddie, and it could be suggested that with the unfortunate death
of Colonel Fry on May 31,[289] so too ended the talk of court-martialing
these men.

John Fraser's accountability at the Forks was a little more excusable. He
had originally accepted the commission with the stipulation that he could
remain at his house on Turtle Creek to conclude his business, but as Colonel
James Innes stated, "He was sent for before the Fr. Landed, but refused to
his Duty, which angered the people here."[290] Despite all the resentment,
Washington changed his tune and felt that Fraser's role was still crucial
with the Virginia Regiment. On August 20, 1754, he wrote to Governor
Dinwiddie suggesting not animosity toward him but rather a promotion:

*If your Honour sho'd think proper to promote Mr. Peyronney, we shall be
at a loss for a good Disciplinarian to do Adjutant's Duty, w'ch requires a
perfect knowledge of all kinds of Duty. I shou'd therefore take it extremely
kind if you wo'd be pleas'd to confer the Office upon Mr. Frazier, who, I
think, I can full answer for, let his former conduct be what it will.*[291]

William Trent, on the other hand, never seemed to rid himself of his
tarnished reputation. Over the next few years, he would defend himself
"against Governor Dinwiddie's Malicious Attempts and Aspersions against
his Character and Credit."[292] In fact, it would set the stage for what became
one of the boldest and controversial acts in William Trent's life as a gentleman
and a man of business.

Chapter 9

VOLUNTEERS ANYONE?

Almost one month later, the situation for Trent worsened. Already accused of negligence at the Ohio, on May 18, 1754, Trent's men were accused again of refractory behavior[293] from when they arrived back at the Inhabitants on April 25, 1754, and refused to obey orders. Looking closely at the months preceding, were these men truly in the wrong for disobeying orders and dispersing? After all, William Trent and his men were more than just lowly backwoodsman or farmers. Yes, they were freelance opportunists seeking adventure and wealth, but more importantly, they were businessmen first.

Clearly, it may have been the reason why these men refused to serve under Washington for anything less than the two shillings per day they had received. As Trent had explained, after he received the packet of papers from Dinwiddie on February 10, they were militia volunteers or militia raised on a different footing.[294] A sense of déjà vu for Trent permeated—just like with his company that served under him for the Crown and for Pennsylvania in June 1746, once again he had been the commander of Virginia's first raised troops.[295] Ironically, Trent sailed to England in 1748 to justify reimbursement that time, as well for lack of payment for volunteered service.[296]

At the Historical Society of Pennsylvania in Philadelphia, the author in his research came across an interesting letter from William Trent to James Burd on July 7, 1754, penned from the "Potomack" or near the New Store in Frederick County, Virginia. Trent would not only describe an account he heard from those retreating to the Inhabitants from the Battle of Fort Necessity, but he would also elaborate further on the refusal to join

Fort Necessity National Battlefield today. *Courtesy of Wikimedia Commons.*

Washington for less pay by complaining about being mistreated at the Forks: "The Government used me ill, not paying my men agreeable to the footing I raised on so they had neither me nor my Men with them."[297]

Unfortunately, with just instructions to protect the Forks of the Ohio at all costs and no enlistment money or letters of credit compensating them in advance for future labor and provisions, Trent carried out orders as he saw fit. They had built the storehouse at Redstone Creek for the Ohio Company and had almost completed an Ohio Company fort.

To him, in those earlier months, the governor had made his true motives quite clear. Being factor of the Ohio Company, Trent was to purchase extra provisions and pay the men and himself with accumulated funds from the Ohio Company. Like he would tell Edward Ward at the Forks and a few years later in his Remarks, "[I]t was no matter so the country was secured for His Majesty, which was his view who was at expense of the fort, as he had orders from the Ohio Company to build a Fort and none from the Government to build any."[298]

Further support of this comes from the journal of the House of Burgesses of Virginia and what was *not* found in those specific papers. After the author read carefully through the submitted petitions by soldiers or their widows, he found not one individual ever submitted a claim for reimbursement or lack of funds for those months from January through April 1754 while serving under William Trent. The reason being that like Trent had promised, he paid each artificer and trader the 2 shillings per day from the day they enlisted. For example, Trent was a captain, and captains were paid 8 shillings[299] per day as per the Virginia Assembly. So, to figure exactly when Trent got paid was to start from when he was first commissioned as a captain on January 26, 1754, until his men arrive back at the New Store on April 25, 1754, and disbanded. So, as Trent was commissioned for eighty-nine days and being paid 8 shillings per day, he made 712 shillings. Divide that by 20 since there were 20 shillings in an English pound and the answer is 35.6, or as it would be written 35 pounds and 6 shillings, about the exact amount Trent would claim he was paid by the Ohio Company whenever his financial accounts were reviewed.[300]

Trent's second in command, John Fraser, was commissioned a lieutenant for seventy days from when Trent arrived at Turtle Creek on February 14 until his men dispersed on April 25. He was paid 4 shillings[301] per day for a grand total of 280 shillings. Once again divide by 20, and he was paid 14 pounds.

Edward Ward was next, and since he was an ensign, he was paid 3 shillings per day from February 12 until the day he rode to Williamsburg on April 25. So, commissioned for seventy-two days, he was paid 216 shillings, or 10 pounds 8 shillings.

Finally, from February 15 to April 12, 1754, those fifty-two men[302] recruited by William Trent plus the twenty or so artificers or carpenters who left the New Store were paid the first raised volunteer rate of 2 shillings per day (according to their enlistment day) until they disbanded on April 25. Together with the full pay of Fraser and Ward, it totaled the 4,444 shillings, or 222 pounds 18 shillings, that equaled the actual amount found in the Ohio Company books.[303]

Trent, in fact, kept such accurate financial records that it was brought up years later that even though the Ohio Company had financed this expedition in its entirety, its debt of reimbursement for 665 pounds 16 shillings[304] was still outstanding in 1757. In other words, an outstanding bill was owed to the Ohio Company, and according to its attorney, John Mercer,[305] there was only one individual held responsible for its repayment in full. Unfortunately, this individual was none other than the governor of Virginia, Robert Dinwiddie.

Trent was at a crossroads. No man had ever taken legal action against his own province's governor, regardless of the circumstances, let alone been awarded a disclosed amount. The proposed act might even be considered treasonous. Besides, with an already tarnished reputation, if he challenged Dinwiddie and lost, the consequences as a businessman and gentlemen would be disastrous.

Time was also a factor. It was well known that Dinwiddie's term as lieutenant governor was ending, and he would soon be setting sail on the next ship to England if the weather was promising in November 1757,[306] so he had to hurry. After conferring once again with John Mercer, Trent decided to act on the good grace of His Majesty and take action. As Dinwiddie was in York, Virginia, Trent arranged a warrant to arrest the governor before he sailed out of the colonies.

Thus, the trial known as *William Trent v. Robert Dinwiddie* was born and would drag on for three long years. Over the course of the trial, Trent submitted every financial record in the Ohio Company books so that the court could see what was potentially owed.

There is not known many specific details of the trial since records have been lost or were burned, but one letter does shed some light on the fateful outcome. On November 8, 1760, George Mercer, a friend of William Trent's, wrote to him:

> *I am just returned from WmsBurg, where I had the Pleasure to be present at your Trial with Govr Dinwiddie, where I may assure You that all his malicious Attempts and Aspersions agt. Your Character and Credit were sufficiently cleared up both to the Court and Jury....*[307] [Mercer would continue, mentioning the verdict was awarded in Trent's favor for £800 and felt excited for his friend, adding,] *I give you Joy of this Piece of real Justice.*[308]

Against seemingly unfavorable odds, Trent had won—not only in the name of the Ohio Company but also, and most importantly, for his honor against Dinwiddie and all other propaganda recently slandering his reputation. He also thanked both George Mercer and Colonel Washington for their assistance in acquiring witnesses to support his good character.[309]

The repayment of this debt went directly to the Virginia House of Burgesses, and it became a matter of debate as to how much of the 800 pounds should be recovered through a public levy. A public levy was basically an additional tax on all tithable persons[310] so that the General Assembly could pay off its accumulated debts. In this case, the committee involved at the House of Burgesses on April 8, 1761, agreed that the 291 pounds, 5 shillings and 10 pence[311] that covered the pay and provisions for Trent and his men would be paid by the "publick."[312] The accrued interest awarded at the trial in Williamsburg, though, was to be excluded, since it was determined that the transaction or agreement of interest was "between the said Lieutenant-Governor and Council and the said Trent."[313]

It is relatively unknown, at least record-wise, if the Ohio Company or William Trent ever received this amount awarded. Regardless of the future, now he could bask in the newfound glory as the gentleman and Indian trader who took down the Virginia governor all by himself.

Chapter 10

THE TRUE NAME OF THE FORT

fter defending himself and his actions for what transpired in those months from January to April 1754, William Trent's victory over Robert Dinwiddie was bittersweet. It also didn't hurt that two of Dinwiddie's main supporters finally voiced their displeasure toward the lieutenant governor as his term was concluding. President of the Executive Council William Fairfax voiced his concern by declaring first that the governor should have king and country at heart whenever he acted, pointing out that "the Great and important business of the Ohio we have always confidered in a National light not as Virginians but as Britons."[314] Obviously it was a subtle way of saying that Dinwiddie had other motives as to why the expedition to build an outpost at the Forks of the Ohio failed from the beginning.

Although not apparent at the time, Colonel George Washington also finally brought to light what the others had whispered about ever since the Forks of the Ohio was captured by the French. Writing to John Campbell, Earl of Loudon and commander in chief of all His Majesty's forces in North America[315] from Fort Cumberland on January 10, 1757, Washington proclaimed his past grievances over the past three years. In this letter, he complained specifically that the failure to possess the Forks of the Ohio came due to failure to act sooner:

Yea, after I was sent out in December 1753[316] *and brought convincing Testimony even from themselves, it was thought to be fiction and Scheme to promote the Interest of a private company (by many Gentlemen that had a share in Government).*[317]

This private company was obviously the Ohio Company, in which Washington, surprisingly, owned no shares, but Dinwiddie was a prominent member along with several other members of his own council and the House of Burgesses.

It was true that the governor had cautiously protected his interests in the Ohio Country while allowing such Virginia Regiment grievances about lack of pay and clothing to fall on deaf ears, even at one time calling them "ill timed Complaints."[318] Meanwhile, the Ohio Company financed the rest of the expedition since Trent purchased provisions and stores from Winchester[319] and had his artificers build a storehouse on Redstone Creek and a fort at the Forks of the Ohio.

One question remains, haunting both researchers and scholars alike. From the day they all arrived at the Forks of the Ohio, was there ever a true name of this Ohio Company fort that Trent was ordered to build? According to authors Charles M. Stotz[320] and William A. Hunter,[321] the unofficial name was just "Trent's Fort," since Ensign Ward or even Trent himself never presented an actual name of the outpost in his writings. Hunter even argued the reason for being an unnamed fort was because it was nothing more than a storehouse surrounded by palisades, like the Ohio Company store they had built back in February.[322]

Now, as was discussed earlier in this book, it was a little more than just an "ill constructed house," as it was later described in the "Detail of Indian Affairs 1752–1754," but there were two instances when the name "Trent's Fort" was used when speaking of this outpost. In the first instance, word had reached Philadelphia on May 3, 1754, of Ward surrendering at the Forks, and the message relayed on the sixth was that an "Account of the French Army of 4,000 French with 18 pieces of artillery appearing before Trent's Fort and its surrender to them on the 17th April."[323] Unfortunately, this is an unreliable source at best, since the number of French and artillery estimated in this secondary account is highly exaggerated in comparison to the primary accounts of the actual number.

The only other time it was known or described as "Captain Trent's Fort" was in a letter George Washington wrote, ironically on this same date, May 6, 1754, to Governor James Hamilton. A small postscript at the bottom of the letter read, "James Foley the express, says he left Mr. Washington at the new store on Potowmac, about one hundred thirty miles from Capt. Trent's

Fort at the Mouth of the Monongahela on Saturday April 27, 1754."[324] Once again referring to it as "Trent's Fort" or "Capt. Trent's Fort" doesn't make a name official; it merely identifies a location or key point occupied by the commander, in this case Trent, since no other account has ever been found of other individuals calling it "Trent's Fort" formally.

Even so, it was Governor Dinwiddie who had a proposal as to what the fort should be called, or what he wanted to call the fort (since it was mentioned after Ward's surrender to French). In a letter dated September 23, 1754, to Horace Walpole,[325] a member of British Parliament, Dinwiddie wrote, "In compliance with His M's Com'd, I raised a Co. of Men and some artificers, and sent them to the Ohio to build a Fort in his M'y's name and to call it Fort Prince Geo."[326] Prince George was the grandson of King George II and would later be George III, whose rule over the Thirteen Colonies would later lead to the American Revolution.

So, since the fort was never completed and there was no evidence declaring that it was called "Fort Prince George" other than anyone besides Dinwiddie, we can safely assume that this also cannot be the fort's official name.

Fortunately, there is one account that can put forth a more reliable name than either Trent's Fort or Fort Prince George. Rightfully so, as it came to light when an indemnity bond[327] suit was filed by George Croghan in March 1767 concerning an all-too-familiar sum of money won in a particular lawsuit called *William Trent v. Robert Dinwiddie*. As Ohio Company financial records were brought forward, it was Thomas Cresap who testified to Ohio Company attorney James Tilghman[328] all the details kept in the "Exact State of the Books Kept by Capt. Wm. Trent."[329] The few statements in the beginning of his letter were of particular interest:

> *As Capt of a Company four or five Months as he was directed by Dinwoodie to Build a Fort at the Mouth of Monongahalia and not being furnished with money by the Govr he was Obliged to make use of the Company's money as well as Goods Such as Blankets, Guns, Powder, Lead &to pay the Workman and furnish them with Provisions for that Purpose as appears in the Company's Books Charged to the Government of Virginia and Fort St George So called in the Company's Books.*[330]

Even though the original Ohio Company books kept by William Trent have never been found, Thomas Cresap was the most credible source to have knowledge of what was written in them. After all, his account of the situation at the Forks corroborated exactly with Trent's statement that the

King George II, by Robert Edge Pine, 1759. *Courtesy of Fort Ligonier in Ligonier, Pennsylvania.*

governor intentionally sent no money, forcing Trent to utilize the high cash flow of the Ohio Company funds. Cresap also was an eyewitness to both sides since he was a member of the Ohio Company and also the itinerant[331] who delivered orders and a commission to Trent at Redstone Creek from Robert Dinwiddie.[332]

Yet Cresap's significant indication of the outpost being named Fort St. George raises curiosity. To the author's knowledge, no other accounts exist mentioning this specific name, so why call it Fort St. George? The most obvious reason was that St. George was the patron saint of England, and the red cross formed in his honor adorns the Union Jack flag of Great Britain in 1754. Another point to consider is the day Trent and his men, staying eight miles away at Turtle Creek, traveled to arrive at the Forks. Coincidentally, that day, February 17, also fell on a Sunday, or the Sabbath. So, with the gathering of the chiefs of the Six Nations and the nearby Delaware tribe with traders from all over, what could be more fitting to welcome everyone's arrival than a prayer from the Book of Common Prayer to "christen" the site of the new fort and possibly record its name, just as Washington conducted to the visiting native families at the Great Meadows after Fort Necessity was finished on June 2, 1754. The chosen prayer could also have been a more widely known one that would bless their current situation against the threat from the north, the French. Perhaps a prayer such as this one: "Help me to overcome the Enemy, Lord Jesus and teach me how to protect myself with ever-increasing faith. Saint George, pray for me. Amen."

That's just a snippet of the full prayer, but nonetheless it's relevant to those devoted to the Church of England such as Trent.[333] "A Prayer to St. George 'the Victory Bringer'" could be, in theory, a reason why the outpost took that name. The name could have also been obtained from a recent event of Trent's former military service in July 1746. After only a month stationed in Philadelphia, he had offered a monetary reward[334] to those who brought back any of his recent deserters and to meet them at the "Sign of St George."[335] Although there is no definitive reason or evidence for why it was called Fort St. George in that account, it can certainly be recognized as the only "true" name that was recorded officially in the Ohio Company books by Trent.

THESE FOUR MONTHS DISCUSSED over the course of this book served as a catalyst. What transpired at the Forks on April 17, 1754, set events in motion that forever changed history and the notable players who were affected by it.

One such affected individual was a newspaper editor and publisher named Benjamin Franklin.[336] When word arrived in Philadelphia on May 3, 1754, that Edward Ward had surrendered the Forks of the Ohio to the French on April 17, Franklin sent a brief note to Pennsylvania colonial agent Richard Partridge.[337] In this letter, he expressed being greatly concerned

The "Join or Die" political cartoon created by Benjamin Franklin that appeared in the *Pennsylvania Gazette* on May 9, 1754, after hearing of Ensign Ward's Capitulation at the Forks in Philadelphia. *Courtesy of the Library of Congress.*

about the current well-being of the colonies but also enclosed in his letter an emblem of his own creation to end "the present disunited State of the British Colonies." The original emblem also appeared in Franklin's newspaper, the *Pennsylvania Gazette*, on May 9, 1754, and became known as America's first political cartoon.

Serving as a rallying cry to unite the colonies together by having each colony "Join or Die," Franklin's broken segmented snake laid the foundation for a future unified nation. This "Join or Die" cartoon was recycled twenty years later, but this time against the armies and tyranny of King George III.

Metaphorically, it could be said that the men of William Trent who braved the winter of 1754 to build a fort were just like these thirteen colonies. Staying together behind those freshly cut logs, they displayed a fine example of words later spoken to unite all the colonies: "We must indeed all hang together or most assuredly we shall all hang separately."[338]

Epilogue

UNFORTUNATE DEPARTURE

From the moment Trent left his men on March 17, 1754, he would never see the Forks of the Ohio the same way again. For the next four years, the French outpost Fort Duquesne would stand strong in place of Trent's outpost, even fending off the biggest threat from British forces when General Braddock and his detachment were defeated just eight miles away[339] on July 9, 1755. Trent's world was changing—it had already changed the moment the French interrupted the construction of the unfinished Fort St. George.

It wasn't until Brigadier General John Forbes[340] and his army approached from the east that the Forks of the Ohio fell back into British hands. Fiercely outnumbered, the French wisely destroyed their magazines and abandoned the burned ruins of the fort, retreating northward to Venango. Forbes and his army arrived at the Ohio on November 25, 1758, having followed the path and advice of their chief Indian interpreter, William Trent, who now served under the province of Pennsylvania. The next day, the fallen Fort Duquesne would be given the name "Pittsbourg" by General Forbes in honor of British Cabinet member and later Prime Minister William Pitt.[341] Trent along with Captain Edward Ward[342] would be on hand to witness what they had hoped to accomplish four years earlier.

On July 4, 1759, as the French and Indian War was nearing the end and leaning heavily in Britain's favor, Trent, Ward and George Croghan (now deputy agent to the superintendent of Indian affairs[343]), found themselves once again in conference with the Indians of the Six Nations, Shawnees,

Plaque dedicated to the exact site of Fort Duquesne at Point State Park in Pittsburgh, Pennsylvania. *Courtesy of the author.*

Delawares and Wyandots[344] at the Forks of the Ohio. Their lighting and smoking the pipe of peace was convincingly hopeful to renew and brighten the chain of friendship, as the British promised the natives to soon drive the French out.

Unfortunately, the natives hopes for a stable coexistence were soon dashed, as British settlers came into the region in great numbers after 1759. Trent and Ward were among them, taking residence.[345] After running the store at the garrison, Trent eventually became the militia commander there when the broken peace turned violent on May 29, 1763. That day, three men came in from Colonel William Clapham's residence[346] near Swiegly Old Town giving an account that "one of his men, two women and a child were murdered by the Wolfe[347] and some Delaware Indians about two o'clock the day before."[348]

More reports came in afterward that outposts were burned at Detroit and Sandusky,[349] leaving not one person alive, and others noted that just one hundred miles to the north, Venango had been left in ashes. Then, on June 24, 1763, according to Trent's journal:

William Pitt the Elder, by George Knapton, circa 1748–50. *Courtesy of Fort Ligonier in Ligonier, Pennsylvania.*

The Turtle's Heart[350] and Mamaltee a Chief came within a small distance of the Fort, Mr McKee[351] went out to them and they made a Speech as Ligonier was destroyed, that great number of Indians were coming and that out of regard to us, they had prevailed on 6 Nations not to attack us but give us time to go down the country and they desired we would set of immediately.[352]

After consulting with his commander,[353] Trent returned to them with a message. Before the Delawares left Fort Pitt to return to their chiefs, Trent gave them a parting "gift" that he mentioned in his journal: "Out of the regard to them, We gave two Blankets and an Handkerchief out of the Small Pox Hospital, I hope it will have the desirous effect."[354] To just what desired effect this example of biological warfare played a role in the native population, the matter is debatable even today. It was known, however, that despite being the bearer of the "infected blankets," Turtle's Heart was still unaffected because five years later he represented the Delaware people at the Treaty of Stanwix, for which Trent recorded the minutes on October 24, 1768.

Following Pontiac's War,[355] Trent tried to regain the losses of lands and goods not only from the recent Indian uprising in 1763 but also from the French and Indian War. Unfortunately, it could not have come during a worse time, and the trial victory over Dinwiddie in 1760 would be the pinnacle of Trent's life and influence.

As negotiations ended the bloody conflict with the Indians, the valued land known as the Ohio Country, including the Forks of the Ohio, became the land of insurmountable debt to those traders such as Trent. The newly claimed lands and imports meant new taxes in the colonies, and a new conflict was beginning to appear on the horizon. Traders like William Trent and George Croghan still were not reimbursed in full for land and supplies lost to the French and Indians since 1752, and now these former employees of a once lucrative land company were financially ruined. Together, they became simply known as the "suffering traders."

Trent would sail to England on their behalf, as the squabbling with Britain would continue in May 1769, and despite encouraging news from the British Parliament to begin a new colony called Vandalia,[356] fighting had broken out in Massachusetts against the Crown and stirred up the colonies. The American Revolution had begun, the first of eight long years of hostilities, seemingly unraveling everything Trent had tried to build. When Trent returned to America on June 5, 1775, his world was at war and everything was confusing. Fort Pitt was now called Fort Dunmore.[357]

For thirty years, Trent would pursue restitution, but to no avail, eventually succumbing to poor health and debt-seeking creditors while staying with friends in Philadelphia on December 1, 1784.[358] Like the fort that he had attempted to build in 1754 at the Forks of the Ohio, Trent's efforts to shape the postwar Ohio Valley were destroyed by powerful forces outside of his control. As a result, Trent slowly faded from the scene and into total obscurity,

View of the present-day Forks of the Ohio, aka Pittsburgh, Pennsylvania, from atop West End Overlook. *Courtesy of the author.*

for even his place of burial remains a mystery today.[359] Consequently, as no landmarks or statues bear his name within the city limits today except for a single street,[360] the firsthand accounts of Trent's forgotten endeavors remain and clearly define him as one of the true founding fathers of the city and settlement known as Pittsburgh.

PLACE NAMES AND THEIR PRESENT-DAY NEIGHBORING COUNTERPARTS

Forks of the Ohio/Mouth of the Monongahela	Pittsburgh, Pennsylvania
Fort Le Boeuf/Fort de la Rivière au Boeuf	Waterford, Pennsylvania
Gist's Settlement/"Monongahela"	Mount Braddock, Pennsylvania
The Great Meadows	Farmington, Pennsylvania
Logstown	Baden, Pennsylvania
Lower Shawnee Town	South Portsmouth, Kentucky
Mouth of Beaver Creek	Rochester, Pennsylvania
Mouth of Chartier's Creek/Shurtees Creek/Der Rocher	McKees Rocks, Pennsylvania
Mouth of Pine Creek	Etna, Pennsylvania
Mouth of Redstone Creek	Brownsville, Pennsylvania
Mouth of Turtle Creek/John Fraser's Cabin	North Versailles, Pennsylvania
Murdering Town	Harmony, Pennsylvania

New Store Tract/Ohio Company Factory	Ridgeley, West Virginia
Paxtang/John Harris's farm	Harrisburg, Pennsylvania
Peter's Creek	Clairton, Pennsylvania
Pick Town/Pickawillany	Piqua, Ohio
Shannapin's Town/Shannopin's Town/Village of the Loups	30th Street in Strip District of Pittsburgh, Pennsylvania
"Skipton"/Cresap's/Shawnee Old Town	Old Town, Maryland
Swiegly Old Town/Oswegle Bottom	West Newton, Pennsylvania
Venango	Franklin, Pennsylvania
Will's Creek/"The Inhabitants"	Cumberland, Maryland

BIOGRAPHICAL SKETCH OF CAPTAIN WILLIAM TRENT

William Trent was born in Philadelphia, Pennsylvania,[361] or possibly Trenton, New Jersey, the son of Pennsylvania Supreme Court justice William Trent and Mary Coddington. His older half brother, James,[362] was a Queen's Scholar[363] at Westminster School in 1714[364] and later attended Balliol College at Oxford in 1717.

In the summer of 1719, his family moved to an eight-hundred-acre plantation along Assunpink Creek and the Falls of the Delaware River in New Jersey, naming the settlement Trent's Town. From as early as 1735 to 1742 or 1743, he worked as an apprentice to merchant Edward Shippen III of Philadelphia. He worked as a clerk and kept books for Shippen's frontier trade depot in Shippensburg in 1744 and 1745. It was also this year, on October 7, 1745, that he purchased in Pennsylvania his first piece of land: 354 acres along the Conodoguinet Creek in East Pennsboro Township.

On June 9, 1746, he alongside John Deimer, John Shannon and Samuel Perry were issued by Governor George Thomas to raise one hundred men each within the province of Pennsylvania for an expedition into Canada during King George's War. The next spring, in April 7, 1747, he and Lieutenant Proctor were ambushed by French and Indians near Captain Philip Schuyler's house at Saratoga but were able to rally and drive them off. This was also the same year he joined a partnership with George Croghan and Richard Hockley. Late in the year 1748, he sailed for London to purchase Indian trade goods and ask for compensation for previous service in King George's War. When he returned in the spring of

1749, he became a justice of the peace in the Cumberland County Court of Pleas in Pennsylvania on March 10, 1749.

Residing in Middleton Township in 1750, he partnered once again with George Croghan and was assisted in the fur trade by Croghan's half brother, Edward Ward. In 1751, he was also a Cumberland County representative in the Pennsylvania Assembly. At the Treaty of Logstown in 1752, he was chosen to deliver presents to the Twightwees, who resided on the Miami River at Pickawillany. Leaving on June 21, 1752, he arrived almost one month later to find the Twightwee village burned and only two English traders, Andrew McBriar and Thomas Burney, having escaped with their lives. Late in this year, he also became factor of the then prominent land speculation company the Ohio Company after its previous factor, Hugh Parker, had died the year before.

In 1753, while residing on the New Store tract at the mouth of Will's Creek in Frederick County, Virginia, with his wife, Sarah, he delivered presents to the Six Nations at Logstown in July along with trader John Owens. After viewing the proposed Ohio Company fort site at the Forks of the Ohio in August, he joined Colonel William Fairfax and ninety-eight Indians at the Treaty of Winchester on September 10, 1753. He also spent the better part of the year as the justice of the peace in Frederick County, Virginia.

On January 30, 1754, he arrived at the mouth of Redstone Creek with fourteen horses carrying supplies to join the twenty artificers who had begun building a fortified storehouse in the name of the Ohio Company. Four days before, Governor Robert Dinwiddie of Virginia had officially commissioned him a captain and ordered him to recruit one hundred volunteers from Augusta and Frederick Counties to build a fort alongside Colonel George Washington and his detachment. On February 10, Thomas Cresap delivered these papers officially to him and headed to John Fraser's cabin at Turtle Creek to await word from the Half King.

Trent arrived at the Forks of the Ohio on February 17 to meet the chiefs of the Six Nations and began a treaty. After the treaty negotiations ended on March 7, he began to mark out the layout of the fort and had the Half King lay the first log of one of the buildings. As supplies and men were depleting, he left the Forks on March 17, leaving a plan of defense for his ensign, Edward Ward, since his lieutenant, John Fraser, had stayed conducting business at his house on Turtle Creek. Later, in November 1754, he acted as chief interpreter with Andrew Montour for Colonel James Innes at a treaty with the Ohio Indians at Fort Cumberland.

In 1755, while serving as a member of the Governor of Pennsylvania's Council and after General Edward Braddock's forces were defeated in July 1755, Trent was elected an officer in the Provincial Service of Pennsylvania to guard his home and the inhabitants at the mouth of Conococheague Creek.[365] Two years later, in 1757, he was the secretary to George Croghan and the superintendent of Indian affairs, William Johnson. It was also the year the Ohio Company was owed reimbursement for the financing of the expedition to the Forks of the Ohio from January to April 1754, and Trent decided to sue Governor Robert Dinwiddie for the £800 owed.

In 1758, he was on the Forbes Expedition as the chief scout for the Indians, and it was his advice of the path to Bouquet's breastworks on September 29, 1758, to General John Forbes that was used to reach Fort Duquesne. As the French and Indian War was ending, in November 1760, Trent received the surprisingly favorable verdict over Dinwiddie and was awarded the full amount specified at the trial. Over the next three years, he ran a private shop with Levi Levy under the firm of Simon and Franks near Fort Pitt, and when it was threatened by the outset of Pontiac's War, he moved into the garrison. During the outbreak in 1763, he was commissioned a major[366] and commanded the militia of Fort Pitt. Alongside Swiss commander Simeon Ecuyer, he gifted blankets to the Indians infected with smallpox from the garrison hospital.

By 1768, he had attended the Treaty of Stanwix along with George Croghan and William Johnson and was granted the tracts of land to supplement losses from 1754 and 1763. The initial group he founded and named was the Indiana Company. To next get approval from Great Britain for this land grant and proposed fourteenth colony, in 1769 he moved his family from Carlisle, Pennsylvania, to Nottingham Township in Burlington County, New Jersey, on a seven-hundred-acre farm on the Delaware River just two miles south of Trenton. On May 25, 1769, he arrived in England under the name of the Grand Ohio Company, or Walpole Company, to seek approval for this colony, "Vandalia." Years would pass, and despite positive news from the Court of St. James's, he didn't return until June 5, 1775, when the colonies were on the brink of war against the Crown.

In July 1776, Trent attended the Treaty of Pittsburgh to speak of the western lands with George Croghan, Edward Ward, Thomas Smallman and George Morgan. Later, in 1780, he joined the New Jersey Assembly representing the Burlington Council. During the next three years, he conducted meetings on Indiana Company business in Philadelphia at the Indian Queen Tavern.[367] He also spent the year beginning on January

4, 1783, as a vestryman for St. Michael's Episcopal Church in Trenton, New Jersey.

His old age and sickness began to get the better of him by January 1784, as he signed over his power of attorney to one of his business partners, Samuel Wharton, and then later to fellow St. Michael's Episcopal Church vestryman Elijah Bond of Trenton on June 1, 1784.[368] One month later, he moved to Philadelphia just before he wrote his last will and testament on July 6, 1784. The last remaining years he spent paying off creditors and debts accumulated as he stayed with friends while succumbing to an illness in the city.[369]

Over the course of his life, he and his wife, Sarah, would have six children. William was born opposite the mouth of Will's Creek in Virginia on May 28, 1754, and was baptized by Chaplain John Hamilton of the Virginia Regiment. Ann was born in Lancaster, Pennsylvania, on October 20, 1756, and was baptized by Reverend George Craig. Martha was born in Lancaster, Pennsylvania, on October 24, 1759, and was baptized by Reverend Thomas Barton. Mary was born in Carlisle, Pennsylvania, on December 3, 1762, and was baptized by Reverend William Thompson. Sarah was born in Carlisle on November 29, 1764, and was baptized by Reverend William Thompson. John was born in Carlisle on April 21, 1768, and was baptized by Reverend William Thompson. His will was finally probated on May 2, 1787, thus ending the life of a man seemingly important yet unfortunately forgotten through time and history.

CONFIRMED MEN WITH WILLIAM TRENT AT THE FORKS OF THE OHIO, FEBRUARY 17, 1754, TO APRIL 17, 1754

A fter careful research, the author was unable to locate the entire list of Trent's men who volunteered to partake in that arduous journey from the Inhabitants to the Forks of the Ohio. However, after poring over numerous primary accounts around that time or somewhat after, there were several names of those men found and confirmed officially to be under Trent's command or attending the Forks during this time span. Their names and brief bios are listed here.

THE OFFICERS OF TRENT'S COMPANY

JOHN FRASER (1721–1773). Fraser arrived in Pennsylvania at age fourteen and apprenticed under Swiss gunsmith Jacob Dubs of Lower Milton Township in the Lehigh Valley. A former gunsmith at Venango for twelve years, he was forced to flee south to the mouth of Turtle Creek in the summer of 1753 on the Monongahela River. Trent chose him as his lieutenant and second in command to oversee the fort building. He remained at his cabin at Turtle Creek to conduct business with his partner, James Young, despite pleas for assistance when the French came down the Ohio on April 17, 1754. Afterward, he was chosen as adjutant of the Virginia Regiment. Later, he became justice of the peace of Bedford County and died there in 1773.

Interior of present-day St. James Episcopal Church, circa 1820, in Lancaster, Pennsylvania. *Courtesy of the author.*

EDWARD WARD (1726?–1793). Ward was half brother of George Croghan, who used to assist Trent with furs and goods at his brother's cabin at East Pennsboro in 1750. He was chosen as ensign despite inexperience at military leadership. His depositions in 1754 and 1756 would be vital to knowing what happened in those waning months before they capitulated the outpost at the Forks. On May 28, 1758, he married the former Hannah Sample Silvers at St. James Episcopal in Lancaster, Pennsylvania, the daughter of Samuel Sample, who would own a publick house in Pittsburgh in the late 1760s. Later, he would join Trent and his brother again on the Forbes Expedition in 1758. He would live most of his life and final days within the city limits of Pittsburgh.

TRENT'S MEN

JACOB ARRANTS. An Indian trader and member of Trent's Company, Arrants was later hired by Colonel George Washington at the Inhabitants for his mastery of the Indian languages and knowledge of the Forks of the Ohio. After the Battle of Fort Necessity, he was captured and forced to march naked by foot to Fort Duquesne and then by way of Fort Niagara to Montreal. His whereabouts after are unknown.

SAMUEL ARSDALE (1722–?). Arsdale was a member of Trent's Company and accompanied Edward Ward to Turtle Creek to talk with Lieutenant Fraser when word reached them of French coming down the Ohio. His surname was spelled "Asdill" in Edward Ward's Deposition of 1754 and "Isdale" upon the return of the men who fought at the Great Meadows on July 3, 1754. He carried goods to Lower Shawnee Town and Venango for George Croghan in 1756. He was later listed on the roster as "Samuel Easdale" for Captain Andrew Lewis's Company in 1757, with height listed as five-foot-seven and age as thirty-five. His name last appears on the roster again of Captain Andrew Lewis in September 1758 right before their disastrous assault near Fort Duquesne with General James Grant.

ROBERT ROBERTS. An Indian trader and private soldier of Trent's Company, Roberts lost goods when the French and Indians attacked and burned Pickawillany on June 21, 1752. He accompanied Edward Ward when he and the Half King accepted the terms from the French commandant on April 17, 1754.

EDWARD LUCAS (1710–1777). A member of Trent's Company who, like Jacob Arrants, was skilled in Indian languages, Lucas assisted Washington after they returned to Will's Creek. He resided on a Frederick County plantation called Cold Spring on the Potomac River near present-day Shepherdstown, West Virginia.

Grave site of Trent's Company member and Indian trader Edward Lucas (1710–1777) at Lucas Family Cemetery at Elmwood in Shepherdstown, West Virginia. *Courtesy of the author.*

THOMAS DAVISON. A member of Trent's Company, Davison was mentioned in Ward's Deposition as traveling to Turtle Creek to ask Lieutenant Fraser to come to the fort when they received word the French were coming in four days.

JOHN DAVIDSON. An Indian trader who resided at Logstown, Davidson was the preferred interpreter of the Half King. He traveled with Major George Washington on his journey to Fort Le Boeuf in 1753, and it was he who confirmed that the French would be down in four days from Robert Callender.

GEORGE CROGHAN (1718–1782). Croghan traded as early as 1739 on Lake Erie and was the half brother of ensign Edward Ward. He was the business partner of William Trent when they bought land on Conodoguinet Creek in what was then Lancaster County in 1745. He stayed at the Forks of the Ohio to help Trent interpret the message from the Six Nations, eventually buying a horse and leaving the Forks just after Trent on March 23, 1754. He is buried at St. Peter's Episcopal Church in Philadelphia.

The grave of Indian trader George Croghan (1720–1782) at St. Peter's Episcopal Churchyard in Philadelphia, Pennsylvania. *Courtesy of the author.*

ANDRÉ MAYNARD. A Frenchman captured with two others near the mouth of Redstone Creek in June 1755, Maynard was sent to Fort Duquesne, where he deposed that he and two others were looking for personal sundry items they had left when Trent's men had constructed it from late January to February 10, 1754.

JOHN FAULKNER. An Indian trader and personal hired hand of William Trent's, Faulkner declared that he had lost thirty-one horses and mares when the French took the Ohio and was forced to leave them behind the next morning after the capitulation on April 17, 1754.

JOSEPH CAMPBELL. An Indian trader, Campbell had a trading house near the Forks of the Ohio and the newly constructed outpost in 1754. He traded with the Half King when he resided at Logstown in 1753 and was later killed near Parnell's Knob in September 1754.

THOMAS CRESAP (1694–1787). An Indian trader and surveyor, Cresap was both an employee and member of the prominent Ohio Company. Known

The grave of Ohio Company member and Indian trader Thomas Cresap (1694–1787) along the C&O Canal overlooking Lock 69 in Oldtown, Maryland. *Courtesy of the author.*

as a "border ruffian" and the "Maryland Monster," he accompanied Christopher Gist to explore Ohio Company lands in 1751 and 1752. He resided at Shawnee Old Town, about fifteen miles from Will's Creek, and it was he who delivered the official commission and orders to William Trent at the mouth of Redstone Creek on February 10, 1754. It was also his letter to James Tilghman on May 20, 1767, that stated that the fort was recorded in the Ohio Company books as "Fort St. George."

CHRISTOPHER GIST (1706–1759). A prominent Indian trader and explorer of the Ohio Company lands from 1750 to 1752, it was Gist whom Dinwiddie recommended to Washington to guide him north of Will's Creek to Fort Le Boeuf in 1753. He was present at the initial treaty with the Six Nations at the Forks on February 17, 1754, and tried to later assist Ward when he and some of Trent's men went back to the storehouse at Redstone Creek to find more supplies. They would not return before April 17, 1754, and would find no more supplies at the storehouse at Redstone Creek. He would eventually succumb to smallpox on the road between Winchester and Williamsburg on July 25, 1759.

JOHN OWENS (1700?–1778). An Indian trader and resident of Logstown, Owens had several children with the daughter of the Half King. He was present at the Logstown council on June 6, 1752, and assisted William Trent with delivering his first caravan of presents from Governor Dinwiddie to the Indians at Logstown on July 11, 1753. After the French took the Forks of the Ohio on April 17, 1754, he lost fifteen horses and a canoe, in addition to a horse lost at the Murdering Town.

NEHEMIAH STEVENS. An Indian trader, Stevens was an employee of the Lowrey brothers Lazarus and James. He was captured near Gist's Settlement on April 23, 1754, after the rest of Trent's men left Redstone Creek and headed for the Inhabitants.

PAUL PEIRCE (1716–JUNE 7, 1794). An Indian trader, Peirce was partnered with John Finley and William Bryan and lost goods on the Wabash River and lower Ohio Country when the French attacked Pickawillany on June 21, 1752. He also had two trading houses on the Forks of the Ohio in 1752 and 1753 and at Muskingum. He is buried at Big Spring Presbyterian Churchyard in Newville, Pennsylvania.

Grave of Trent's Company member and Indian trader Paul Peirce (1716–1794) at Big Spring Presbyterian Church Cemetery in Newville, Pennsylvania. *Courtesy of the author.*

ELIZABETH WILLIAMS. An Indian trader and employee of the Lowrey brothers, Williams was the only confirmed woman trader at the Forks of the Ohio. She was also captured near Gist's Settlement on April 23, 1754.

ANDREW MCBRIAR. One of only two English traders who fortunately escaped the attack on Pickawillany before it was burned on June 21, 1752, McBriar would see his luck run out on April 23, 1754, when he was one of four captured near Gist's Settlement and sent to Fort Duquesne.

JOHN KENNEDY. An Indian trader for the Lowrey brothers, Kennedy was unlike the other three captured near Gist's Settlement. He was severely wounded in the altercation on April 23, 1754, and left in the care of English John until he was able to walk again. Later, he was taken to Fort Duquesne with the others.

JAMES FOLEY. An itinerant and express rider between Colonel Washington and William Trent at the Forks of the Ohio, Foley might have been the person who delivered the first news of Ward's capitulation to Washington on April 19, 1754. He was mentioned in Washington's letter on April 27, 1754, estimating that the Inhabitants was 130 miles from Captain Trent's Fort.

DANIEL HART. An Indian trader, Hart resided in Lancaster County, Pennsylvania, and was present at the Forks of the Ohio in March 1754. On March 2, 1754, he sold a brown gelding natural pacer named Woolabarger to George Croghan.

FRENCH OFFICERS

CLAUDE-PIERRE PÉCAUDY DE CONTRECOEUR (DECEMBER 28, 1705–DECEMBER 13, 1775). An officer in the French colonial regular troops (Troupes de la Marine), Contrecoeur was the commander of the expedition to expand in the Ohio Country. He and his force of about five hundred to six hundred men landed at Shannopin's Town three miles north of the Forks on April 16, 1754, and that night, he wrote the summons to whom he assumed would be William Trent at the Forks of the Ohio the next day. His compassion was shown when he invited Edward Ward to dinner the night of the seventeenth and allowed the rest of Trent's men to leave the Forks unmolested back to the Inhabitants.

FRANÇOIS-MARC-ANTOINE LE MERCIER (DECEMBER 22, 1722–1798). An artillery officer and engineer, Mercier designed the plan for Fort Presque Isle on Lake Erie and Fort de la Rivière au Bœuf on French Creek. On April 17, 1754, he personally handed Contrecoeur's summons to Edward Ward and told him that he had one hour to comply. His suggested threat to take the fort by force and use of his pieces of artillery decided the fate of Trent's men for him.

THE NATIVES

HALF KING (1700?–OCTOBER 4, 1754). The Half King's name was signed as "Tanareeco" on May 1, 1747, but he was called the Half King by the English and Tanarisson by the Six Nations. Though adopted by the Seneca, he was born a Catawba and resided at Logstown with a hunting cabin on Beaver Creek. It was he who first suggested to the Ohio Company to build an outpost at the Forks of the Ohio. He was chosen to accompany Christopher Gist and George Washington as they headed north to visit the French commandant on French Creek in 1753. At the Forks of the Ohio as leader of the Six Nations, he laid the first log of one of the structures being built and argued incessantly with the French whenever they claimed the Forks as theirs. A scuffle ensued, and although a French officer was shoved to the ground, nothing materialized that day. Later, he would aid Washington in beginning the first shots of the French and Indian War at a rocky bower later called Jumonville Glen after the French ensign he killed on the morning of May 28, 1754. Unfortunately, sickness would take him, and he died on John Harris's farm in Paxtang on October 4, 1754.

Present-day site of John Harris's farm in Paxtang and now currently the city of Harrisburg, Pennsylvania. *Courtesy of the author.*

Monacatootha. An Oneida chief also known as Scarouady. (Ensign Ward spelled his name as Serreneatta in his deposition.) Along with the Half King, he supported the Ohio Company's decision to build a fort at the Forks of the Ohio. He was also the one who suggested to Ward to build a stockade around the buildings and put up wooden palisades to protect them before the French came down the Allegheny River on April 17, 1754.

Andrew Montour (1720–1772). The son of the famed "Madame" Montour, Andrew Montour was also known as Sattelihu and French Andrew because he was of Oneida and French ancestry. He assisted George Croghan at the Forks of the Ohio on February 17, 1754, and accompanied William Trent to view the proposed site of the fort at the Forks of the Ohio on August 27, 1753. His services at the Forks with Trent and Ward led him to be later commissioned a captain of eighteen traders at the Great Meadows in July 1754.

The Owl. Delaware chief and ally to the French, the Owl resided in a village named Owl's Town in what is now present-day Coshocton County, Ohio. He accompanied Captain Le Mercier to the Forks of the Ohio on April 17, 1754, and stood with him when he handed the summons to Ensign Ward and the Half King. After Trent's men vacated the Forks, he followed them to near Gist's Settlement and tried to buy goods off them. After an altercation ensued, he would bring four of them back to Fort Duquesne to be sold.

English John. Delaware Indian and ally to the French, English John traded with the Ohio Company. He was present at the Forks of the Ohio on April 17, 1754, when the French offered their terms to Ward and then followed Trent's men from the Ohio to Gist's Settlement with the Owl. After an altercation resulted over traded goods, the Owl captured and took three of them back to Fort Duquesne while he waited for the fourth, John Kennedy, to recover from his injuries.

COMMISSION OF WILLIAM TRENT AND OFFICIAL ORDERS ON JANUARY 26, 1754

Official Records of Robert Dinwiddie, 1751–58, vol. 1, pages 55–57.

On January 16, 1754, Lieutenant Governor Robert Dinwiddie received his report from the young emissary George Washington, who had just returned from Fort Le Boeuf. After reading the French commandant's reply, Dinwiddie immediately suggested to the Governor's Council a captain's commission for William Trent to recruit one hundred men. The date of the official commission was January 26, 1754, and his official orders were delivered to Trent by Thomas Cresap at the mouth of Redstone Creek on February 10, 1754.

COMMISSION OF CAPTAIN WILLIAM TRENT

Rob't Dinwiddie Esq'r His Majesty's L't Gov'r Com'd'r in Chief and Vice Admiral of his Colony and Dom'n of Virg'a—

To WM. TRENT, ESQ'R:
   Whereas certain Persons pretending to be Subjects of his most X'n Majesty the King of France, and that they act by his Como. have in a hostile Manner invaded the Territories of our Sovereign His M'y King George the 2d King of Great B. &c. and have comitted divers Outrages

and Violences on the Persons and Goods of His M'y's Subjects, in direct violation and infract'n of the Treaties at present subsisting between the two Crowns, and Whereas these Acts of hostility and depredations have been perpetrated in that Part of His Majesty's Dom's w'ch are under my Gov't; In order therefore to the Preservation of the Peace and Good understanding between the two Crowns and the Preservation of our Sovereign's undoubted rights, and the Protection of his Subjects as much as in me lies, I have thought fit to appoint and by Virtue of the Power and Authority to me given as Com'd'r in Chief of this Colony, I do hereby constitute and appoint You Wm. Trent Esq'r to be Com'd'r of such and so many of His My's Subjects not exceeding 100 Men as You can imediately raise and enlist, and with the s'd Comp'a and the Assist-ance of our good and faithful Friends and Allies the Ind's of the Six Nat's and such others as are in Amity with them and Us, to keep Possession of His M'y's Lands on the Ohio and the Water thereof and to dislodge and drive away, and in case of refusal and resistance to kill and destroy or take Prisoners all and every Person and Persons not Subjects of the King of G. B. who now are or shall hereafter come to settle and take Possess'n of any Lands on said River Ohio, or on any of the Branches or Waters thereof. And I do hereby require the s'd Men who shall so en-list themselves and every————of them to obey You as their Com'd'r and Capt'n &c. and You are to constitute such and so many Officers under You as the Service shall require, not exceeding 1 Capt. and 1 Lieut't.

Given under my Hand and the Seal of the Colony at W'msburg the—— Day of Jan'y in the 27 Year of His M'y's Reign, annoq Dom. 1754.

GOVERNOR DINWIDDIE TO WM. TRENT, ESQR.

SIR:

   Y'r Letter of the 6th Curr't I rec'd from Maj'r Washington, from his report, Informat'n and Observat's I find the French intend down the Ohio to build Forts and take Possession of the Lands on that River, w'ch I w'd very earnestly prevent. And as You think You c'd this Winter, if properly impower'd to do so, I therefore inclose You a Capt's Com'o to raise 1oo Men in Augusta and in the exterior Settlem'ts of this Dom'n and a blank Com'o for You to choose a suitable Lieut. to Co-operate with You. Y'r Comp'a will be in the Pay of this Gov't agreeable to the Assembly. Maj'r Washington has a Com'o to raise 100 Men, with them he is to join You and I desire You may march Y'r Men out to the Ohio where a Fort is propos'd to be built.

When You are there You are to protect and assist them in finishing the Fort and to be on Y'r Guard ag'st any Attempts of the French. I doubt not the Woodsmen You may enlist will be provided with Guns &c., I have appointed Maj'r Carlisle of Alexandria a Commiss'y of Stores and Provisions, he will supply You accordingly with what Necessaries You may want and in case of want of Guns I have sent some to his Care to be delivered to the Com'd'rs of either of these Compa's giving receipt accordingly for them. As You have a good Interest with the Ind's I doubt not You will prevail with many of them to join You in order to defeat the Designs of the French in taking their Lands from them by force of Arms. The Ho. of Burgesses are to meet the 14th of next Mo. w'n I hope they will enable me to send out 400 more Men early in the Spring to Y'r Assistance. I wrote to the neighbouring Gov'rs for their Aid and Assistance on the present Emergency and I am in hopes they will supply a good Number of men &c. I have some Cannon come in—ten I send up to the Comissary at Alexandria—they carry four Pound shot—I fear there will be a difficulty in carrying them out—as You are acquainted with the Roads, I shall be glad of Y'r Advice therein, and comunicate the same to Maj'r Carlisle. You see the Confidence and good Opinion I have of Y'r Capacity and Diligence w'ch I hope You will Exert on this Occasion by keeping a good Comand and strongly engaging our friendly Ind's to be on the Active. Provisions will be difficult to send regular Supplies. Mr. Washington says one Mr. Frazier can provide large Qu'ty of Venison, Bear, &c. I desire You may write him to get what he can. When You have compleated Y'r Comp'a send me a List thereof and the time of their enlisting and the Places of their Aboad. I wish You Health and Success in the present Expedition and am Sincerely

    S'r Y'r h'ble Serv't

Appendix III

DEPOSITION OF EDWARD WARD ON MAY 7, 1754

Public Record Office, Colonial Office Papers, 5:14, 193–99.

Edward Ward, ensign in William Trent's Company, was the commander of Trent's men when they capitulated their outpost at the Forks of the Ohio on April 17, 1754. The next morning, on April 18, Ward rode ahead to deliver the bad news to Colonel George Washington at the mouth of Will's Creek. At Will's Creek, he borrowed Washington's horse and saddle and rode to Williamsburg to deliver his report to Virginia governor Robert Dinwiddie. Ward arrived in Williamsburg, Virginia, on May 4 and deposed the following report.

> *Ensign Ward's Deposition before the*
> *Governor & Council ye 7th of May 1754*

> *Mr. Edward Ward Cap't Trents Ensign deposes and makes Oath to the following Particulars, That the French first appeared to him at Shanopins Town about two Miles distant from the Fort the 17th of April last, that they moved down within a small distance from the Fort, Then landed their Canoes, and marched their men in a regular manner a little better than Gun shot of the Fort. That Le Mercier a French Officer sent by Contrecoeur the Commandant in Chief of the French Troops came with an Indian Interpreter, called by the Mingoes the Owl, and two Drums, one of which served for Interpreter between Le Mercier and him; Le Mercier presently*

deliver'd him the summons by the Interpreter, looked at his watch which was about two, and gave him an hour to fix his Resolution, telling him he must come to the French Camp with his Determination in Writeing. He says that half an Hour of the time allowed him, he spent in Council with the Half King, who advised him to acquaint the French he was no Officer of Rank or invested with powers to answer their Demands and requested them to Wait the Arrival of the principal Commander. That at the time the Summons was deliver'd to him, the Half King received a Belt of Wampum much to the same purpose. That he went accompanied with the Half King, Rob' Roberts, a private Soldier, and John Davidson as an Indian Interpreter, that the Half King might understand every word he spoke at the French Camp, That he there address' d himself to the Chief Commander Contrecoeur and expressed himself agreeably to the above mentioned advice of the Half King, That the French Commander told him he should not wait for an Answer from any other person, And absolutely insisted on his determining what to do that Instant, or he should immediately take Possession of the Fort by Force. That he then observeing the number of the French, which he judg'd to be about a Thousand and considering his own weakness being but Forty one in all, whereof only Thirty three were Soldiers, Surrender'd the Fort with Liberty obtained to march off with everything belonging thereto by Twelve o'clock the next Day. He says that night he was Oblieg'd to encamp within 300 yards of the Fort with a Party of the Six Nations who were in Company with him, That the French Commander sent for him to Supper and ask'd many Questions concerning the English Governments, which he told him he could give no Answer to, being unacquainted with such affairs, That the French Commander desired some of the Carpenters Tools, offering any money for them, to which he answer'd he loved his King and Country too well to part with any of them And then retired. That next morning he received the speech from the Half King to the Governour, And proceed'd with all his men towards Redstone Creek where he arrived in two Days; and from thence marched to Wills's Creek, where he met with Coll' Washington and informed him of every particular which had happened, That Coll' Washington thought fit to send back one of the Indians to the Half King with a Speech and to Assure him of the Assistance which was marching to him; And by the advice of a Council of War dispatch'd him an Express to his Honour with the other Indian and an Interpreter, judging him the most proper Person having been appointed by the Half King. He moreover adds that four days before the French came he had an Account of their comeing, and saw a Letter that John Davison wrote to

Rob' Calender an Indian Trader to confirm the truth that they were to be down by that time. That the Day following he sent a Copy of Davison's Letter to Cap' Trent who was then at Wills's Creek, and went directly himself to his lieutenant who lived Eight or Ten miles up Monongahela from the Fort at a place called Turtle Creek, it was late at night when he got there. Accompanied by Robert Roberts, Thomas Davison, Samuel Asdill, and an Indian, and shew'd him the Letter, of which he sent a Copy the next Day to his Captain. The Lieutenant told him he was well assured the French would be down, but said what can we do in the Affair. The morning after he sent for the Half King, and one of his Chiefs named Serreneatta, who advised him to build a Stockade Fort, That then he asked his Lieutenant if he would come down to the Fort, to which he Answer'd he had a Shilling to loose for a Penny he should gain by his Commission at that time, and that he had Business which he could not settle under Six Days with his Partner; That he thereupon answer'd he would immediately go himself and have the Stockade Fort built. And that he would hold out to the last Extremity before it should be said that the English had retreated like Cowards before the French Forces Appeared, and that he knowing the bad consequences of his leaveing it as the rest had done would give the Indians a very indifferent opinion of the English ever after. He further says he had no Orders from either his Captain, or Lieutenant how to proceed, and had the last Gate of the Stockade Fort erected before the French appeared to him. That he was credibly Informed by an Englishman who attended the French Commandant that they had 300 Wooden Canoes, and 60 Battoes and had four men to each Canoe and Battoe, that they had also Eighteen Pieces of Cannon three of which were nine Pounders. That the Half King stormed greatly at the French at the Time they were oblieged to march out of the Fort and told them it was he Order'd that Fort and laid the first Log of it himself, but the French paid no Regard to what he said.

Sworn to by the abovemention'd Ward before
The Governor in Council
Teste the 7th May 1754.

Appendix IV

DEPOSITION OF EDWARD WARD
ON JUNE 30, 1756

Historical Society of Pennsylvania, Etting Collection, Ohio Company Papers.

Two years had passed since Edward Ward, former ensign under Captain Trent, gave his deposition to Governor Robert Dinwiddie on May 7, 1754. Ward was commissioned a captain in service of Pennsylvania on May 22, 1756, and this time gave another deposition to Samuel Smith, a district justice of Cumberland County, Pennsylvania. Ward's deposition was given on June 30, 1756, and provided a more detailed account of the capitulation of the Forks of the Ohio in the spring of 1754.

THE THIRTIETH DAY OF JUNE IN THE YEAR OF OUR LORD, ONE THOUSAND SEVEN HUNDRED AND FIFTY SIX.

Before me Samuel Smith Esq, one of his Majesties Justices, Edward Ward of the said County Gent. And upon his solemn oath did depose and declare, that he this Deponent was Ensign of a Company of Militia under the Command of Captain William Trent in the Pay of the Government of Virginia That at the Time said Captain Trent received the Governor of Virginias Orders, he was at Redstone Creek about thirty seven miles from where Fort DuQuesne is now built and was erecting a Store House for the Ohio Company. That when said Trent received the Governors Instructions to raise a Company he despatched Messengers to several parts of the Country where the Indian Traders lived, there being no other Inhabitants in that part of the Country except four or five Families who had lately settled there and were upwards of Sixty Miles from the inhabited Part of the Country. That one of said Messengers, employed by Captain Trent came to the place where this Deponent was and informed him of said Trent having received such Instructions and upon the Half King and Monacatoochas receiving advice that said Trent had orders to raise a Company of men, they sent him a Message to come immediately and build a Fort at the Forks of the Monongahela and Ohio and that they would assist him as soon as they could gather the People. On receiving such Message said Trent got Rafts made and every other thing necessary for his march and accordingly did march with what few men he had then raised in order to meet the Indians as requested. That the said Capt Trent had then erected but not quite finished a strong square Log house with Loop Holes sufficient to have made a good Defence with a few men and very convenient for a Store House was paid for by Captain Trent, who at that time was Factor for the Ohio Company and had orders to build said Store House to lodge Stores which were intended for the Building a Fort where Fort Du Quesne now stands for the Ohio Company, which Store House was soon after completed by Workmen employed by said Captain Trent for that purpose. That Captain Trent marched from Redstone Creek to the mouth of the Monongahela where a number of Indians of different Nations met him, at which Time and place this Deponent was present having met Captain Trent on his march and received his commissions as Ensign from him. Captain Trent on meeting with the Indians made a speech to them and delivered them a present, which was sent by the Governor of Virginia. After the Treaty was finished Captain Trent laid out the Fort and cleared the Ground and got some logs squared, upon which the Chiefs of the Six Nations then present went with us to the ground and laid the first log and said, that Fort belonged to the English and them and whoever offered to prevent the building of it they the Indians would make war against them. That Captain Trent left the Inhabitants and crossed the mountains in the middle of winter and brought a quantity of flour and Indian Meal with him on horseback over the mountains with great difficulty. Those Mountains being impassible in winter if deep snows happen. The first concourse of Indians that gathered at that time during the Treaty were maintained by Captain Trent out of the Flour and Indian Meal, he took with him a large quantity of goods to pay for it to the Delaware Indians, they being the only Indians who lived adjoining, to the place where the Fort was building, and could not be prevailed upon to hunt, tho' often applied to and offered great prices for any kind of meat they could bring in, even seven shillings and sixpence for a Turkey. At this time the Indians were much inclined to the French, but were afraid to declare in their favour. We lived upon Flour and Indian Meal chiefly, while, it lasted, sometimes getting a Turkey at a very extravagant rate. After the Flour and Meal was gone we lived chiefly upon Indian Corn, all that could be got we purchased. Mr Gist sent word that Major Washington with a Detachment of the Virginia Regiment were on the march to join us and would be with us in a few days and we also received the same account from several other persons. Captain Trent waited a long time, till our provisions got scarce, having nothing but Indian Corn, and even salt to eat with it was scarce, very little of it to be purchased, and the weather so hot the Men were not able to work, having become very weak by having nothing but corn to eat.

Upon this Captain Trent set off for the Inhabitants to try to get some relief and I understand that when he came to his House which was within fifty miles of Winchester near where Fort Cumberland now stands that there was no account from the Regiments nor any Detachment from it nor any provisions sent up there and that said Captain Trent provided a quantity of provisions and was determined to join the Company and wait the coming of the Regiment. That the day before he proposed setting off he received a letter from Major Washington desiring him not to leave the Inhabitants till he saw him as he wanted his advice, and the day they got back to Captain Trents House, they received the news of about eleven hundred Indians and French having come down the Ohio and taken possession of the Fort, our people were building.

And this Deponent further saith he understood that the detachment of one hundred and fifty men of the Virginia Regiment under Major Washington had been but two days at Captain Trent's House before we came in from the Ohio and this Deponent further saith that he found them very ill provided, being obliged to make use of the Flour provided by Captain Trent and that afterwards they were supplied with powder by said Trent and George Croghan, Esq, otherwise they would not have had ammunition to make the least defence, that day the French defeated them. The men under the command of Captain Trent had received no pay but what he paid them. The Government intending to pay them as the soldiers belonging to the Regiment were paid, though they were raised as Militia, agreeable to the Act of Assembly then in force.

The want of their pay and the unsafe march made them refuse to serve upon any other footing. And this Deponent further saith that there was no

Fort but a few Palisades he ordered to be cut and put up four days before the French came down. And this Deponent further saith that he often heard Captain Trent say that he did not want a commission. That his business was better than any commission and what he did was to serve his Country and that if he could get the Fort finished he would be satisfied. And this Deponent further saith that the Soldiers who were willing to work were paid by Captain Trent at the expence of the Ohio Company and that he had often heard Captain Trent say; it was no matter so the Country was secured for His Majesty, which was his view who was at the expense of the Fort, as he had orders from the Ohio Company to build a Fort and none from the Government to build any. And this Deponent further saith that the Indians gave Captain Trent encouragement that they would join him and drive the French off the Ohio; but upon finding how backward the Governor of Virginia was in sending Troops, the Indians told Captain Trent that for what men he had with him they looked upon them as no addition to their strength, as they had long lived among them, looked upon them all one as themselves, but if the Virginians joined them, which they saw no signs of, then they would join heartily, and that the Half King desired Captain Trent to go to the Inhabitants and forward the troops and provisions. And this Deponent further saith that after Captain Trent, left the Fort in order to go to the Inhabitants, and hurry out the Troops and Provisions and recruit his Company that Mr Gist came to the Fort and desired him to send some men with him to bring down a quantity of Provisions which were laying at Redstone Creek. That this Deponent then sent a number of men up the Monongahela for said Provisions. That he understood afterwards there were no provisions there, that before the men who were sent for them got back, the French came down and obliged this Deponent to surrender, he having no place of Defence but a few Pallisadoes which he had ordered to be put up four days before upon hearing the French were coming down and that he had no Provisions but a little Indian Corn and but forty one soldiers and Workmen and Travellers who happened to be there at the time and the French Eleven hundred in number, And this Deponent saith he saw several pieces of Cannon pointed at the Fort within musket shot but could not tell the number, but was afterwards told by the Indians there were nine pieces of Cannon.

Sworn to at Carlisle the
Thirtieth day of June 1756 Edward Ward
Before me Sa. Smith

EXPENSE ACCOUNT OF THE GOVERNMENT OF VIRGINIA TO WILLIAM TRENT DATED APRIL 8, 1754

Virginia (Colony) Colonial Papers, 1630–1778, accession 36138, State Records Collection, Library of Virginia, Box 147, Folder 44.

On March 17, 1754, William Trent left his men at the Forks of the Ohio to return to the Inhabitants for more supplies and men. The following account by Trent, recorded on April 8, 1754, at Will's Creek, listed the following expenses that began when Trent gathered presents for the Six Nations in Winchester, Virginia, in September 1753.

> *For Carriage of Fourteen Horses loaded with Powder, Lead, and Flints from Col. Cresaps to Ohio River at 2 Pistoles a Load is 20 Pistoles......a 21/6......&30.2.0*
>
> *For Carriage of the Powder, Lead, and Flints from Winchester to the Col......7.0.0*
>
> *For 12 Deer Skins......a3/......1.16.0*
>
> *For 9 Doe Bear Skins......a6/......2.14.0......4.10.0*
>
> *For 19 ¼ yards purple half thicks for Bags to put the Powder in......a 2/9 a yard......2.12.11 ¼*
>
> *For 3500 Black Wampum a 40/per M......7.0.0*
>
> * 300 White ditto......a3/2 per Ct......0.9.6......7.9.6*
>
> *{NB 3000 of the Black Wampum and the 300 White was used in one belt}*

For one making the Belt and the Leather to make it with......2.0.0

For One Peice of Matchcoat to wrap the Powder with......7.10.0

For 1 Gun, 1 Pistol and Matchcoat gave to one of the Six Chiefs of the Six Nations who Came down from the Upper Towns, as he Came upon Business he brought no Arms with him, he said it was hard for him to go home without Arms as he should run a great Risque as he was Obliged to go through the French to Warn their People from Amongst them......3.15.0

For 1 Case of Neat Pistols gave to the Half King and Monacatootha and 2 fine Ruffled Shirts and 2 plain Shirts for themselves and Wives Pistols 2.10/ Shirts 3.10.0......6.0.0

These given as a particular Present sent by the Governour to them

For and Express sent for Mr. Andrew Montour to come to me to Ohio to deliver the Speeches paid by Coll. Cresaps......2.12.0

Carried Over......72.11.5 ¼

Brought Over......72.11.5 ¼

NB. There is no Carrying out Powder without Skin Wrappers when I had them of my own I made no Charge these I was Obliged to buy I used two Pieces of Matchcoats for Inside Wrappers, one peice being the outside ones in the Bundles were damaged which I gave to the Indians and with which I charge the Government there is no Such thing as Carrying Powder without damaging without...............

For four Pounds paid Coll. Cresap for his going Express with the Governours Letters to me at Red Stone Creek......4.0.0

76.11.5 ¼

Accepted this 8ᵗʰ April 1754

William Trent

Appendix VI

ACCOUNT OF THE BATTLE OF THE GREAT MEADOWS IN A LETTER FROM WILLIAM TRENT TO JAMES BURD DATED JULY 7, 1754

Historical Society of Pennsylvania, Shippen Papers XV, page 119.

On July 3, 1754, Colonel George Washington and Captain James Mackay were forced to surrender their small outpost at the Great Meadows to the French. The Virginia Regiment and South Carolina Independents returned to Will's Creek, and the following account was told to William Trent, who still resided on the New Store tract near the mouth of Will's Creek. This letter mentioning this account was written to James Burd along with his reasons why Trent and his men refused to join Washington's detachment at the Great Meadows after the capitulation of the Forks of the Ohio.

Powtomack July the 7th 1754

On third of this Instant about 10 o'clock in the morning the French Army consisting of about One Thousand French and Indians attacked our Troops consisting but of about three hundred & fifty men, the fight lasted till dark, it rained hard all day, our Guns got wet so that they found themselves not in a fit Condition to renew the fight & the next Morning the French called out to our People to parley, they were glad of it and marched out of the Fort Trenches the next morning with Drums beating & Colours flying but they suffered the Indians to plunder our People of everything contrary to the Articles of Capitulation we had about Sixty killed & wounded private Men, Several officers wounded only second lieut to the Independent Company from Carolina French had about two hundred killed &wounded the French and Indians of All Nations, & will have all the Indians in the Woods unless our People exert themselves they cannot do anything in this part of the World without the other Collonies assist them. You may expect to hear of nothing but continued Murders committed by the French Indians who may be immediately expected down upon the back Inhabitants the French sent me word they intended to come & see me soon they make no doubt of being Masters of all America—The Government used me ill, not paying my men agreeable to the footing I raised on so they had neither me nor my Men with them I am in haste

Sir Your friend & humble St
William Trent

N.B. The Fort was only made and able to contain
about 100 men.
Lt. Poulson is safe returned.

GEORGE MASON TO JAMES TILGHMAN, STATEMENT OF WILLIAM TRENT'S ACCOUNT WITH VIRGINIA, WHILE FACTOR OF THE OHIO COMPANY, ENCLOSING LETTER OF JOHN MERCER DATED MARCH 1, 1767

Historical Society of Pennsylvania, Cadwalader Papers.

While William Trent was the factor of the Ohio Company, he kept accurate financial records that were used and submitted in his trial against Robert Dinwiddie. He was awarded the full sum according to the final verdict. In 1767, after George Croghan filed compensation from this verdict, secretary of the Ohio Company George Mason mentioned these records and the particular ones Trent recorded during his time spent from January to April 1754 building a fort at the Forks of the Ohio. The typed transcription of this letter and of Trent's accounts recorded in the Ohio Company books are listed following.

> *Upon being informed that Mr. Croghan claimed some Credit on his Bond to the Ohio Company for part of the Money recovered by Captain Trent from Governor Dinwiddie, George Mason sent to Mr. John Mercer (who managed the Suit for Captn. Trent desiring a particular Accot. of the matter, and received from Mr Mercer the following Answer and Account.*

(copy)

"Dr. Sir
Your memorandum by my son gave me a good deal of trouble to search for
Captain Trents papers, tho' I was almost certain that they would not turn
to Mr. Croghans advantage any further than by returning an Account of his
which our Assembly refused to allow
"Captain Trents claim for his own £35…4.2 and his Mens
pay in the whole £222…18.0 for provisions for himself and
Men……………………………………………………68.7.9
for going out with the first present, himself £100 Horses £90.16.0
Wampum £16.4.provisions. £11.14.9…Owens…6.11.4 bringing in
Skins
£6.9.0…Interpreter £5.16.0.an Express £5…French Deserters
Express 40/1 247.18.10
Halfthicks 38/9 A ruffled Shirt 15/…one ps. ribbon 9/1 a Skin
for Belts 5/.

"For going out with the second present, himself £50…Horses £37.2.
presents £9.15.0 Wampum £8.9.6 Match Coats £7.10.0
Expresses 126.11.5
£6.12.Skins   for   Belts £4.10 Halfthicks
£2.12.11……………………

———————————

£665.16.0

"Of that sum £321.11.2 was due to himself, and £344.4 to his Men.
He offered me any
"part of what I could recover of it, and I realy believe it would have been
lost, if I had not
"by a good ffee procured Mr. Dinwiddie to be arrested at York. Even
afterward the Court
"put me upon such proof of the Account as they were almost certain I could
not procure
"but meeting Colo. Washington and Colo. Mercer who recommended me
to some other witnesses then luckily in Town and having a good Jury who
resented the Treatment Trent met with; they not only allowed the whole
Accot. but gave such Damages as satisfied me, and therefore I according

126

to Capt. Trents order gave the Ohio Company Credit for the whole
£665.16.0 I hope this will be satisfactory, I am Dr Sir,
Your most Obedient Servant,

John Mercer
March 1ˢᵗ. 1767."

George Mason was at the Expence and trouble of procuring from the Secretarys
office Authentic Copys of all Capt. Trents Accots. & in the Suit with
Mr. Dinwiddie and found them to agree exactly with the above state of
Mr. Mercers except the Article for provisions of £68.7.9 which in the
Office Copy is £70.9.9. but whence this difference of £2.2. arises, is not
apparent This it is presumed will be sufficient to satisfie both Capt. Trent
& Mr. Croghan, that Mr. Croghan is not entitled to any Credits from the
Ohio Company on this Accot. and if by any private agreement between Mr
Trent and Mr Croghan the latter has a right to any part of it (which does
not appear to be the case) from the Papers in the Suits / Capt. Trent ought
to pay Mr. Croghan himself, As Mr. Mercer has given Capt. Trent Credits
for the whole sum to the Ohio Company.

Mr. Croghans Accot. Certificates for which the Virginia Assembly
refused to make him any Allowance are inclosed herewith Mr. Tilghman
will be pleased to return them to me And oblige his most Hble. Servt.

G. Mason

TRENT'S REMARKS IN 1757 PERTAINING TO THE ACCOUNT OF THE OHIO COMPANY FORT AT THE FORKS OF THE OHIO IN 1754 AND THE BURIAL OF LIEUTENANT PETER MERCIER AT THE GREAT MEADOWS IN JULY 1754

In the late summer of 1757, William Trent authored a ten-page document in direct response to attacks of his character that were found in the English translation of *A Memorial Containing a Summary View of Facts, with Their Authorities, in Answer to the Observations Sent by the English Ministry to the Courts of Europe by Jacob Nicolas Moreau.* Being autobiographical reflections of past events, I have named the document "Trent's Remarks 1757." Specifically, in three pages of Trent's Remarks, Captain William Trent goes into explicit detail of when he left his house in January 1754 near the Inhabitants at the mouth of Will's Creek until he arrived at the Forks of the Ohio to begin building the Ohio Company fort. He also discusses when he left the Forks to gather more supplies and the status of Colonel George Washington finally arriving at the Inhabitants. For the first time, a written transcription of these three pages is provided.

The 21 January 1754 I left my own House near where Fort Cumberland now stands with a quantity of Powder lead & flints sent by the Government of Virginia to the Ohio Indians at their repeated request to defend themselves & the English Traders against the attempts of the French who were then marching to attack them.

The 30th I arrived at Monongahela where Redstone Creek empties itself into Monongahela, upon my arrival I sent a Messenger to acquaint the Indians that I had brought them some Arms Ammunition & defend them to meet me at the Mouth of Monongahela that I might deliver them_ I had taken some Carpenters out with me and had a Strong fortified Store House built at the Mouth of Red Stone Creek it being the first Convenient place for laying Stores to be transported by Water to the Mouth of Monongahela When the Ohio Company had given me orders to have a Fort built-/ this is the Store House that the French call the Hangard which they acknowledge they burnt.

The 10th I received a Packet from the Governor of Virginia inclosing me a Commission to raise One Hundred Militia to join the men Coll. Washington who had Orders to raise a Company of Militia likewise- upon receiving the Governors letter I inlisted Some Indian Traders & marched with them from Red Stone Creek to Turtle Creek near to where General Braddock was defeated & Stayed there till I received advice that the Indians were gathering in order to receive the Arms Ammunition &: which the Governor of Virginia had sent by me to them, by the 7th of March I finished all my Business with the Indians that I was charged with from that Government_ during the Course of my transacting the Business I was charged with, the Chiefs of the Indians insisted that I should set the Indian Traders that I had enlisted & the Workmen that I had brought out with me to Work and begin a Fort against the Troops from Virginia should arrive_ At the request of the Indians I set the Carpenters to Work & layed out a Fort and the Chiefs of the Six Nations layed the first log of one of the StoreHouses and declared that this Fort belonged to the English and then in conjunction with the English they would defend it against any Nation that should attack it_ We received an Account that Coll. Washington was on his March and would be there in a few days. I would till the 17 of March in expectation of Coll. Washington coming in order to put in Execution a plan layed between the Indians & myself which must effectively have prevented the French from dispossessing us of the Ohio When I found Coll. Washington was not likely to come so soon as we expected I endeavored to get the Indians to execute the Plan layed between us but they told me as for myself & my Men they did not think we were any addition to their strength from the White People because we chiefly lived in that Country and from the longtime we had lived amongst them they looked upon us as Indians and told me that it sound as if the English did not intend to assist them else they would have had their Men out before that & then insisted I would immediately set off for the Inhabitants & hurry out Coll. Washington with the Troops-We had no provisions for some day.

I had furnished the Men I raised hither to with all necessaries at my own Expense and as I had rec'd neither Arms, Ammunition, Provisions, Money or Letters of Credit from the Government I set of to receive them & raise the remainder of the Men agreeable to the Instructions as everyone was moving of their Effects, there was no more Men to be got in the Country I left my Men at the Ohio the 17ᵗʰ March with the command of my Ensign as my Lieutenant had not joined me. At this time I had finished Storehouse and everything ready upon the Spot for raising another & a large quantity of timber as the Situation things were in why I left there in for the & knew the great advantage it would be for the Troops to be provided with Stores (in a Place where there was no House nigher than two Miles now inhabitants nigher than 20 miles) and have timber ready to raise the Fort against the arrival of Troops that they might immediately have a place of defense I constantly attended the Work from daylight in the Morning till Night as every one Worked & every one seemed to have the good of the Country at heart there was an incredible deal of Work done in the time___ As I was obliged to go up the Monongahela in order to get Provisions to maintain the Men till my return it took me till the 27 March before I got to my House where Fort Cumberland now stands and where I expected to have met the necessary Arms Ammunition & for my Company but upon my arrival there I received a Letter from Coll. Washington dated at Alexandria the 19 March (Alexandria not less than 150 Miles the Waggon Road, lower down the country than where I was) leting me know that he had received orders to march and Convey the Arms & that in 7 or 8 days the wagons would be ready upon learning that Coll. Washington was convoying the Arms &: for my Company I immediately began to provide Provisions to send out to my Men & to recruit the remainder of my Company, the day Coll. Washington came to my House we received an Accot. that the French with 9 pieces of Cannon and 700 men had obliged Mr Ward my Ensign to abandon the Work_ The Virginians having altered their Scheme of raising the Men, mine as they were Militia & raised upon a different footing were discharged when they came in without pay except what I had payed them *myself this was the true State of things when I left Ohio and I understand there was nothing more done to the Fort after I left it, except laying one Log all around, four days before the French came Mr Ward got Intelligence of them and put up some small Pallasadoes to prevent the French from Rushing and at that time I had not more than two days Provisions & not quite fifty men including with the Souldiers, the workmen and travelers that happened to be there at the time_____*

I thought fit to give you a full Account of this Affair as the French have thrown some Reflections on my Character in that Memorial of theres and unless it be just my particular Acquaitance, many believe that there was a good Fort there and that I had delivered it up tho' I was not within a hundred Miles of the Place at the time_ As well as to let the World know what kind of place it was & what force was there at the time of the French Army coming with 700 Men & 9 Pieces of Cannon (this the same Cannon which is at the time at Fort DuQuesne) to attack my People there under the Command of Mr. Ward_____

Also found in "Trent's Remarks" is commentary by Trent pertaining to the aftermath of the capitulation at Fort Necessity in the summer of 1754, including not only a former member of Trent's Company, Jacob Arrants, but also a new native account about the French Indians digging up the body of South Carolina Independent officer Lieutenant Peter Mercier and scalping him after being buried during the night before on July 3, 1754. This written transcription is new primary evidence of a soldier being buried at the Great Meadows.

After the Capitulation the French made and Carried of several English Prisoners, One named Jacob Arrants, so far were they from suffering the English to bring off of their Effects that they allowed the Indians to plunder our People, broke open their Chests and take away such things as the Officers & souldiers could have brought off with them_____

Even the Surgeon's Chest they suffered the Indians to destroy to prevent our wounded from being dressed, they suffered Indians to raise Lt. Mercier of the Kings Troops after he was buried & Scalp him without interfering in the least to prevent it. Coll. Washington had not above 300 Effective Men the day of the Engagement.

ENGLISH TRANSLATION OF THE SUMMONS OF CONTRECOEUR TO ENGLISH ON APRIL 16, 1754

French transcription is in Papiers Contrecoeur, *pages 117–19; English translation is in* History of Pittsburgh and Environs, *vol. 1, pages 263–64.*

On the night of April 16, 1754, in the Delaware village of Shannopin's Town just three miles north of the Forks of the Ohio, Captain Claude-Pierre Pécaudy de Contrecoeur scratched his pen to the paper and wrote out his warning to the English traders whom he had heard were constructing buildings at the Forks of the Ohio. The summons he gave to artillery captain François Le Mercier would be the document he would hand the next day to ensign Edward Ward on the afternoon of April 17, 1754.

A summon by order of Contrecoeur, captain of the companies of the detachment of the French Marine, commander-in-chief of his most Christian Majesty's troops, now on the Beautiful River, to the commander of those of the King of Great Britain, at the mouth of the River Monongialo.

Sir
Nothing can surprise me more than to see you attempt a settlement upon the lands of the King, my Master; which obliges me now, Sir, to send you this gentleman, Chevalier Le Mercier, captain of the Bombardiers, commander of the Artillery of Canada, to know of you, Sir, by virtue of what authority you are come to fortify yourself within the dominions of the King, my Master. This action seems so contrary to the last treaty of peace concluded

at Aix La Chapelle, between his most Christian Majesty and the King of Great Britain, that I do not know to whom to impute such an usurpation, as it is incontestable that the lands situated along the Beautiful River belong to his Christian Majesty.

I am informed, sir, that your undertaking has been concerted by none else than by a company who have more in view the advantage of the trade than to endeavor to keep the union of harmony between the crowns of France and Great Britain, although it is as much the interest, sir, of your nation as ours to preserve it.

Let it be as it will, Sir, if you come into this place charged with orders, I summon you in the name of the King my Master, by virtue of orders which I got from my General, to retreat peaceably with your troops from off the lands of the King (and not to return or else I find myself obliged to fulfill my duty and compel you to it. I hope, sir, you will not defer an instant and that you will not force me to the last extremity). In that case, sir, you may be persuaded that I will give orders that there shall be no damage done by my detachment.

I prevent you, sir, from the trouble of asking me one hour of delay nor to wait for my consent to receive orders from your Governor. He can give none within the dominions of the King, my Master. Those I have received from my general are my laws, so that I cannot depart from them. If, on the contrary, sir, you have not got orders, and only come to trade, I am sorry to tell you that I cannot avoid seizing you, and to confiscate your effects to the use of the Indians, our children, allies and friends; as you are not allowed to carry on a contraband trade. It is for this reason, sir, that we stopped two Englishmen last year, who were trading upon our lands; moreover, the King, my Master, asks nothing but his right; he has not the least intention to trouble the good harmony and friendship which reigns between his Majesty and the King of Great Britain.

The Governor of Canada can give proof of having done his utmost endeavors to maintain the perfect union which reigns between the two friendly princes; as he had learned that the Iroquois and the Nippessingues of the Lake of the two mountains had struck and destroyed an English family towards Carolina, he has barred up that road and forced them to give him a little boy belonging to that family, which was the only one alive, and which Mr Welrich a merchant of Montreal, has carried to Boston; and what is more, he has forbid his savages from exercising their accustomed cruelty upon the English and friends.

I could complain bitterly, sir, of the means taken all last winter to instigate the Indians to accept the hatchet, and to strike us, while we were striving to maintain the peace.

I am well persuaded, sir, of the polite manner you will receive Monsieur Le Mercier, as well out of regard to his business as his distinction and personal merit. As you have got some Indians with you, sir, I join with M. Le Mercier, an interpreter that he may inform them of my intentions upon that subject.

I am with great regard, sir, your most humble and obedient servant. Contrecoeur.

Done at our Camp, 16 April 1754

NOTES

Introduction

1. It was Richard Peters who also wrote on November 24, 1748, about Trent that "before he engag'd in the King's service he carried on the Indian trade successfully in partnership with George Croghan who is one of the most reputable & sensible traders & Trent might by this time have made a fortune but ambition seiz'd him so violently that he broke up the partnership in hopes to be a man of figure in the conquest & settlement of Canada."

Chapter 1

2. The Virginia Company was chartered under King James I on April 10, 1606, and consisted of two joint stock companies that hoped to establish settlements on the coast of North America for England.
3. James Charles Stuart (1566–1625), the son of Mary, Queen of Scots, was king of Scotland as James VI from July 24, 1567, and king of England and Ireland as James I from March 24, 1603, until his death in 1625.
4. The Six Nations of the Haudenosaunee (People of the Longhouse), or Iroquois Confederacy, originally comprised the Mohawk, Onondaga, Oneida, Cayuga and Seneca people. The Tuscarora people were added as the sixth nation after 1722.

5. Thomas Lee (1690–1750) was the Northern Neck proprietor for 6 million acres of land owned by Lady Catherine Fairfax while she resided in England. He was a member of the House of Burgesses and Governor's Council in the Virginia General Assembly.

6. It was the northernmost of three peninsulas (called "necks") in Virginia. Called the "Athens of the New World" because of the rich landowners, the Northern Neck was bounded by the Potomac River on the north and the Rappahannock River on the south.

7. Augustine Washington Jr. (1720–1762) was the second and youngest son of Augustine Washington and Jane Butler. His half brother was George Washington.

8. Lawrence Washington (1718–1752) was a prominent landowner in Virginia and a member of the Fairfax County legislature. The beloved half brother of George Washington, he was the first to live in the house near little Hunting Creek he named after his commander, Admiral Edward Vernon, during the War for Jenkin's Ear.

9. A tributary of the Ohio River and the largest inland waterway in present-day West Virginia, at ninety-seven miles long.

10. The 130-mile-long river flows south to north and joins the Allegheny River to form the Ohio River at the Forks of the Ohio (present-day Pittsburgh).

11. Official Records of Robert Dinwiddie, vol. 1, 17.

12. Christopher Gist (1706–1759) was the son of Zepporah Murray and Richard Gist, a surveyor of the city of Baltimore, Maryland, and was a colonial explorer and surveyor for the Ohio Company from 1750 to 1753. On November 14, 1753, he accompanied a young George Washington into the upper Ohio Country to see the French commandant at Fort Le Boeuf.

13. Christopher Gist's journals, edited by William M. Darlington.

14. One of the largest Indian villages in the Ohio Country, located on the north bank of the Ohio River eighteen miles below the Forks of the Ohio near present-day Baden, Pennsylvania. From April to July 1785, the lands on the Ohio River were surveyed by Daniel Leet for the Second District of Depreciation Lands, and Lots 18 and 19 were marked as "Old Logstown" on his map. Today, these combined lots are now part of the site owned by Old Economy Village that lies on Sixteenth Street between Baden and Economy, Pennsylvania.

15. Pierre-Joseph Céloron de Blainville (1693–1759) was a French Canadian officer in the Compagnies Franches de la Marine who commanded the lead plate expedition into the Ohio Country in 1749.

16. To strengthen French claim in the Ohio Valley, an expedition led by Captain Pierre-Joseph Céloron de Blainville in 1749 was to "mark" French ownership at several mouths and tributaries of rivers. A tin or copper plate with the French royal arms was nailed to a tree, and a lead plate bearing the same insignia was buried in the ground below it. One such original lead plate exists today at the Virginia Historical Society in Richmond, Virginia.

17. A viceroy was a representative or authority figure who spoke on a group's behalf. In this case, it was the Six Nations.

18. The Half King, or Tanarisson (1700–1754), born a Catawba, was an adopted Iroquois chief and speaker for the Indian tribes of the Six Nations. His voice held much influence for those tribes who resided in the Ohio Country. The English referred to him as the "Half King" when addressing him in letters.

19. Many scholars refer to the Half King's Indian name as Tanacharison or Tanaghrisson, but the Half King would make his mark and sign his name as Tanareeco on May 1, 1747. The author chose to use the spelling as it was recorded by Trent, who interacted with him more than anyone. Trent said in his Remarks in 1757 that the Six Nations only called him by his true name, spelled Tanarisson. In a letter dated April 7, 1753, from French commandant Pierre Paul de la Malgue Sieur de Marin to Philippe-Thomas Chabert de Joncaire, he spelled the name similarly, as Thanenhisshon. It must be noted as well that in the *Colonial Records of Pennsylvania*, vol. 5, in the fall of 1753, it is spelled surprisingly as Deharachristion. It can be noted, however, that in the Seneca language, the *D* sound can be mistaken for a *T*, hence the similarity to the scholarly spelling of Tanacharison. The Half King's name is referred to as Thonariss in the Treaty of Logstown of 1752. See the *Virginia Magazine of History and Biography*, vol. 13, 160. Conrad Weiser during his visit to the Ohio in 1748 spelled the name phonetically as Tannghrishon.

20. Another name for the Forks of the Ohio since the mouth of the Monongahela River joined with the Allegheny River to form the Ohio River.

21. The first French fort built along Presque Isle Bay in the summer of 1753.

22. The second French fort built in 1753 along the banks of French Creek and Le Boeuf Creek near present-day Waterford, Pennsylvania.

23. The supply post built by the French in 1754 used gunsmith John Fraser's house near the confluence of French Creek and the Allegheny River

(present-day Franklin, Pennsylvania) after they forced Fraser to flee after residing there for twelve years.

24. George Augustus (1683–1760) was the son of George I and served as King George II of Great Britain and Ireland from June 11, 1727, until his death in 1760.

25. Robert Dinwiddie (1692–1770) was born in Glasgow, Scotland, and was a former merchant who served as the royal lieutenant governor of Virginia from 1751 to 1758.

26. Thomas Fairfax, the 6th Lord Fairfax of Cameron (1693–1781), came into possession of the vast Culpeper family estates in 1719 and was the only Scottish peer who resided in the colonies, owning about 5,282,000 acres in Virginia.

27. This was the date the Governor's Council announced officially that George Washington would be properly commissioned as a major and travel north of Logstown to visit the French commandant.

28. George Washington (1732–1799) was the first child of planter Augustine Washington and his second wife, Mary Ball Washington, born on their Popes Creek estate in Westmoreland County, Virginia. His journal in 1753, written about his mission into the Ohio Country to visit the French commandant at Fort Le Boeuf, would be his first step into notoriety.

Chapter 2

29. *Diaries of George Washington*, 132.

30. Forks of the Ohio, or present-day Pittsburgh, Pennsylvania.

31. The confluence of the Ohio River begins at the Forks, where it is formed from the Allegheny and Monongahela Rivers and continues 981 miles into the Mississippi River.

32. The mouth of Chartier's Creek was the site of a Delaware Indian village and is now near present-day McKees Rocks, Pennsylvania.

33. George Mercer (1733–1784) was a surveyor and one of eight captains of the Virginia Regiment. He was wounded at the Battle of the Great Meadows on July 3, 1754. Later, he was commander and lieutenant colonel of the Second Virginia Regiment in 1758.

34. *George Mercer Papers Relating to the Ohio Company*, 226.

35. Skipton was what Thomas Cresap called his residence at "Shawnee Old Town" after his birthplace of the same name in England.

36. Charles Calvert, 5th Baron Baltimore (1699–1751) was a British nobleman and proprietary governor of Maryland. His territorial dispute with Pennsylvania led to what was known as the Conejohela War, or Cresap's War.

37. One of the largest rivers in North Carolina, it rises in the northwestern part of the state. Gist and his family resided at the time in Wilkes County on the Yadkin River's northern side and just west of the Reddies River.

38. The settlement of Will's Creek was also called the Inhabitants in several primary accounts and is known today as Cumberland, Maryland.

39. Also known as Laurel Mountain (elevation 2,800 feet) in present-day Fayette County, Gist's new settlement was in Mount Braddock, Pennsylvania, alongside present-day Route 119.

40. *Pennsylvania Archives*, series II, vol. 2, 422–25.

41. William Trent (1653?–1724) was born in Inverness, Scotland, and immigrated to Philadelphia sometime after 1682, being listed on the Philadelphia tax list of 1693. He came from a family of merchants and at one time held a prosperous yet questionable business shipping kidnapped children as indentured servants to the colonies with his uncle, Maurice Trent, of Leith, Scotland, and the West Indies. He had four children— Mary, James, Maurice and John—with his first wife, Mary Burge, who died in June 1708. His only child to live into adulthood with his second wife, Mary Coddington, was the eventual Captain William Trent. In summer of 1719, they would move into their house, which still stands today in Trenton, New Jersey. A man devoted to the Church of England, he also became a Supreme Court justice in Pennsylvania and New Jersey until his untimely death on December 25, 1724.

42. Trent's Town is today known as Trenton, New Jersey, and is the capital city.

43. Mary Coddington Trent (January 15, 1693–December 15, 1772), the second wife of Justice William Trent (married on July 20, 1710), was the stepdaughter of Anthony Morris Jr., a Quaker preacher, former mayor of Philadelphia and founder of the Morris brewery, one of the oldest breweries in Philadelphia. She is often confused with being the daughter of Governor William Coddington of Rhode Island, but that Mary Coddington married Peleg Sanford in 1674. Her father was Thomas Coddington, and her grandfather was William Coddington.

44. Anthony Morris (August 23, 1654–October 23, 1721) was born in Old Gravel Lane in the Stepney District of London, England. He was a second-generation merchant who moved to Philadelphia and began a brewery that resided adjacent to Front and Water Street along the

Delaware River. He joined the Society of Friends alongside the founder of the Pennsylvania Colony, Quaker William Penn. His third wife was Mary Howard Coddington (married on January 18, 1694, in Newport, Rhode Island), mother of Mary Coddington Trent.

45. The William Trent House was completed in the summer of 1719 by builders from Philadelphia. It has been suggested that Philadelphia architect and Carpenter's Company founder James Portues was credited with building the Trent House, but there is no sufficient evidence to support this. He is, however, credited with building Christ Church on Second Street and Isaac Norris's Fair Hill Mansion in Philadelphia.

46. These are both weaving terms. For example, if a silk vest such as the Trent vest is "warped," then the silk threads are held longitudinal and stationary in tension on a frame or loom. "Wefting" or "woofing" refers to threads that are transverse and inserted over and under the warp threads.

47. According to his bust and recorded height at Mount Vernon.

48. *George Mercer Papers Relating to the Ohio Company*, 147–48, 439.

49. Allegheny Hill was the range of mountains located about ten miles from present-day Cumberland, Maryland.

50. *Executive Journals of the Council of Colonial Virginia*, vol. 5 (1739–54), 439–40.

51. William Fairfax (1691–1757) was a former collector of customs in Barbados and former governor of the Bahamas. He was a member of the House of Burgesses and president of the Virginia Governor's Council. He was also a vast land agent for his cousin Lord Thomas Fairfax's holdings in the Northern Neck of Virginia.

52. Paul Marin de la Malgue (1692–1753), a veteran of King George's War, constructed Fort de la Rivière au Boeuf (Fort Le Boeuf) and died on October 29, 1753.

53. Near present-day Rochester, Pennsylvania.

54. A river in south-central Ohio that meets the Ohio River in Portsmouth, Ohio.

55. *Executive Journals of the Council of Colonial Virginia*, vol. 5, 440.

56. On April 7, 1747, Captain William Trent and Lieutenant Proctor with forty Pennsylvania men were attacked by a large detachment of French and Indians from Crown Point led by Monsieur Sherbine near Saratoga. At the first firings, eight of his men were killed, but Trent was able to rally the rest of them and drive them off within the hour of it beginning.

57. Old Fort Saratoga was a stockade fort built on the heights east of the Hudson River by Peter Schuyler in 1709 below the mouth of Batten Kill.

58. According to the memorandum of losses during the battle that day, Trent had six men scalped and lost twelve blankets, twenty-three deerskins, fifteen knives, two cooking glasses, gunpowder, musket balls, two waistcoats, tobacco, pipes, Indian meal, thread, leather, chocolate, one pocket pistol and two gun cases.

59. Nehemiah How was captured at his home by Indians near present-day Putney, Vermont, on October 11, 1745. He would later publish the account of his imprisonment in Quebec in 1748 in Boston, Massachusetts, calling it "A Narrative of the Captive of Nehemiah How, 1745–1747." The account would mention on page 54 the prisoners of the skirmish involving Trent on April 7, 1747, and he being mistakenly named as one of the soldiers killed.

60. James Logan (1674–1751) was a former secretary for wealthy Quaker William Penn in 1699, the mayor of Philadelphia in 1722 and a founding trustee of the Academy and College of Philadelphia (known today as the University of Pennsylvania). He was also a former schoolmaster who could have assisted Shippen in furthering Trent's education. Edward Shippen III (1703–1781), born in Boston, was mayor of Philadelphia in 1744 and founded Shippensburg, Pennsylvania. Shippen's mercantile store was near the first wharf built in Philadelphia called Carpenter's Wharf along the Delaware River.

61. For the first time, the author was able to find primary evidence that Trent was Shippen's apprentice. In the Shippen Family Papers at the Library of Congress Under Accounts, 1734–1804, there is a note written in Trent's handwriting dated April 5, 1742, that ends with the phrase "on Accot. of my master Edw. Shippen." In addition, the earliest Trent signatures the author found were either as a witness or on land indentures found between the years 1740 and 1744, alongside accounts made by either James Logan or Edward Shippen.

62. The author recently found in the ledgers of Benjamin Franklin's print shop two entries that shed some evidence on Trent's early schooling as he worked under merchant Edward Shippen. The first was dated June 9, 1738, and was recorded as "Edw'd Shippen, Dr. for Bayley's Exercises, 3.0. Shop Book." The other was a purchase by Trent's mother, Mary, recorded on May 20, 1738, as "Widow Trent, Dr. for Clark Intreyduckshon for Lattin, 5.0. Shop Book." Both of these specific books were common in teaching Latin and grammar to a boy developing an education in a public school or apprenticeship of the period.

63. It was known as the College of New Jersey when it resided in Elizabeth, New Jersey, in 1746, but after moving to Nassau Hall, it is known today as Princeton University.

64. See the Edward Shippen Letters and Papers, 1727–1781 (American Philosophical Society). In these specific papers are correspondence between Edward Shippen and his son Joseph, with letters entirely in French and a letter with trigonometry equations.

65. The land in Lancaster County (now part of Cumberland County) was a tract of 354 acres along the Conodoguinet Creek (near present-day Mechanicsburg, Pennsylvania) that he acquired with George Croghan from William Walker on December 24, 1745.

66. Trent was the justice of the peace in Cumberland County, Pennsylvania, in 1749 and 1750 and also in Frederick County, Virginia, in 1753, when he resided at the New Store Tract on the North Branch of the Potomac River. He was also part of the Cumberland County Assembly in 1751, when he lived on a 244-acre plantation in Middleton Township, near Carlisle.

67. John Fraser (1721–1773) came to Paxtang (near Harrisburg, Pennsylvania) in 1734, apprenticing under Swiss gunsmith Jacob Dubs of Lower Milton Township, and later established a trading house at Venango as early as 1741. After repairing guns and trading for twelve years, he was forced to flee to the mouth of Turtle Creek in May 1753.

68. Andrew Montour (1720–1772), known as French Andrew or Sattelihu, was part Oneida and part French.

69. Present-day Franklin, Pennsylvania, near the mouth of French Creek.

70. Near present-day North Versailles, Pennsylvania, where the mouth of Turtle Creek and the Monongahela River meet.

71. James Young was a former employee of the Ohio Company and business partner of John Fraser in 1753 and 1754.

72. The Half King was not present because he was traveling north to the French forts again to warn them against coming into the Ohio Country in September 1753—that and because Governor Dinwiddie wasn't present either.

73. From "William Trent's Account of Proceedings with Six Nations of Indians and Allies November 17, 1753," Darlington Family Papers.

74. *Executive Journals of the Council of Colonial Virginia*, vol. 5, 443.

75. Ibid., 444.

76. William Trent's Remarks, Native American Collection, Clements Library.

77. Pickawillany or Pick Town was a Miami Indian village built in 1747 on the Great Miami River. The British were given permission and built a trading post where the Piankashaw chief Memeskia (known to the English as Old Briton) lived and traded with the English. On June 21, 1752, a large party of Ottawa and Ojibwa Indians led by Charles Michel de Langlade burned the stockade and storehouse, killing Old Briton for his refusal to support the French.

78. See Appendix V, Governor of Virginia to William Trent, April 8, 1754.

79. As factor of the Ohio Company since 1752, William Trent sold consigned goods, buyers credits and sometimes cash advances to principals prior to the actual sale of the goods. He basically performed the functions of a governor without any other "regular" authorities. He was preceded by Hugh Parker, who was factor until his death in spring of 1751. Coincidentally, Parker worked alongside Trent in the 1740s in Philadelphia, making both factors of the newly formed Ohio Company trained by the merchant Edward Shippen.

80. Skilled craftsman.

Chapter 3

81. *Diaries of George Washington*, 157.

82. Trent's Remarks, 3.

83. Trent's house was near where Fort Cumberland's earthworks sit presently under the current site of Emmanuel Episcopal Church. The Maryland side of the Potomac River was then Frederick County, Maryland, and today is part of Allegany County. His house lay a few hundred yards away opposite this and was on or near the New Store tract in Frederick County, Virginia, and what would be now present-day Ridgeley, West Virginia.

84. Indian trader and the first "factor" or agent of the Ohio Company from 1749 to 1751.

85. Sarah Wilkins (died on March 26, 1801) was the supposed daughter of a Donegal trader and had six children: William (born May 28, 1754), Ann (born October 20, 1756), Martha (born October 24, 1759), Mary (born December 3, 1762), Sarah (born November 29, 1764) and John (born April 21, 1768) with her husband, William Trent. Trent referred to his wife's maiden name, Wilkins, in his will dated April 14, 1775, which he wrote before he sailed from London to Philadelphia on April 21, 1775.

86. *Maryland Gazette*, no. 928, February 17, 1763.

87. Ibid.
88. *Executive Journals of the Council of Colonial Virginia*, vol. 5, 440.
89. Present-day Brownsville, Pennsylvania.
90. Expense account of William Trent, April 8, 1754 (see Appendix V).
91. January 30, 1754, was the day Trent arrived at the mouth of Redstone Creek from the New Store. It took him nine days.
92. Trent's Remarks, 3.
93. Several sources, including the author, have seen George Croghan's own handwriting, and he phonetically spelled it several times as "Crohan." We can only assume it was pronounced this way too.
94. Croghan to Governor James Hamilton, February 3, 1754, *Pennsylvania Archives*, series I, vol. 2, 119.
95. George Croghan died on August 31, 1782. His will was probated on September 3, 1782. William Trent wrote his final will on July 6, 1784, although it was not proven until May 2, 1787.
96. John Davidson was an Indian trader and interpreter at Logstown. A favorite of the Half King, he was chosen in 1753 to accompany George Washington on his mission north to Fort Le Boeuf.
97. The Giahaga Creek that Croghan refers to was the mouth of Cuyahoga River, which empties itself into Lake Erie where present-day Cleveland, Ohio, lies today.
98. Trent's Remarks, 8.
99. Holes in the building were used as windows and firing positions.
100. Journal of Coulon de Villiers, June 30, 1754.
101. Name given to the storehouse at Redstone Creek by the French. It means shed or cache.
102. The French also destroyed Gist's Settlement near present-day Mount Braddock, Pennsylvania, including burning his plantation and the surrounding outbuildings.
103. Louis Coulon de Villiers (1710–1757) was a French military officer and on July 3, 1754, defeated Colonel George Washington at the Great Meadows near present-day Farmington, Pennsylvania. The attack was revenge for the death of his half brother, Joseph Coulon de Villiers, Sieur de Jumonville (famously known as Ensign Jumonville), who was killed in the skirmish at the rocky bower on May 28, 1754, a place we know today as Jumonville Glen. He was the only opponent to ever make Washington officially surrender.
104. James MacKay (1718–1785) was a veteran of James Oglethorpe's regiment and the commanding officer of the South Carolina Independent

Company, which fought alongside George Washington at the Great Meadows on July 3, 1754.

105. Further evidence of bodies lying atop the ground after the battle was confirmed by an unnamed British officer, who wrote on June 25, 1755, as the detachment passed through the Great Meadows almost a year later saying, "There are about 150 Acres of Meadow-land entirely clear; built by Mr Washin[g]ton last Year when he retreated from the French;… There are many human bones all round ye spott; but at present every thing is entirely pulled down."

106. Edward Braddock (1695–1755) was the British commander and general of the disastrous campaign to take Fort Duquesne. On July 9, 1755, he suffered mortal wounds at the Battle of the Monongahela and died later, one and a half miles from Fort Necessity on July 13, 1755. He was buried in the wagon road to prevent looting and desecration by the Indians giving chase, and workers later found Braddock's remains when constructing a road in 1804.

107. Trent's Remarks, 4.

108. See Governor of Virginia to William Trent, April 8, 1754.

Chapter 4

109. Official Records of Robert Dinwiddie, vol. 1, 59.

110. Opposite of what Dinwiddie instructed Trent to do, mentioning nothing whatsoever on acting defensively.

111. Trent's men were still building the storehouse at the mouth of Redstone Creek. This is a supporting statement of this outpost being an Ohio Company fort.

112. *Journal of Captain William Trent, Logstown to Pickawillany, A.D. 1752*, 58.

113. Trent was the one of the acting justices of the peace of Frederick County, meaning he still resided on or near the New Store tract.

114. *Pennsylvania Archives*, vol. 1, 688–89.

115. *Official Records of Robert Dinwiddie*, vol. 1, 57.

116. Ibid., 55.

117. Deposition of Edward Ward, May 7, 1754, PRO Colonial Office, 5:14, 193–96.

118. Deposition of Edward Ward, June 30, 1756, *Ohio Company Papers, 1753–1817*, 26–31.

119. Probably to any nearby areas with able-bodied inhabitants.
120. Trent's Remarks, 9.
121. The author believes that Edward Ward was at his brother's plantation at Swiegly Old Town about twenty-five miles from the Forks of the Ohio and on the way to John Fraser's cabin at Turtle Creek.
122. *Ohio Company Papers, 1753–1817*, 28.
123. According to Paul A. Wallace, author of *Indian Paths of Pennsylvania*, the path ran between two Indian towns: the Shawnee village on the Youghiogheny River near present-day West Newton, Pennsylvania, and, traveling north, the Indian town along the Allegheny River near present-day New Kensington, Pennsylvania. Both were at one time referred to by the name Sewickley Old Town.
124. Present-day West Newton, Pennsylvania, along the mouth of Sewickley Creek, twenty-five miles from present-day Pittsburgh.
125. Trent's Remarks, 5.
126. Scarouady, or Monacatootha, was an Oneida chief at Logstown. He came with the Half King to receive gifts at the Ohio.
127. Hale, *Indian Wars of Pennsylvania*, 139.
128. Ibid., 4.
129. John Fraser lived at Venango from 1741 to 1753.
130. *Official Records of Robert Dinwiddie*, vol. 1, 55.
131. Ibid.
132. Ibid.
133. Volunteers or first raised militia troops were paid two shillings per day, and regular private solders were paid eight pence per day.
134. *Pennsylvania Gazette*, July 31, 1746; September 4, 1746; and September 11, 1746.
135. Horatio Sharpe (1718–1790), a former captain who fought in the Forty-Five Rebellion against the Jacobites, was the royal proprietary governor of Maryland from 1753 to 1768.
136. *Official Records of Robert Dinwiddie*, vol. 1, 116.
137. Cambrick or cambric was a very fine linen used to make neck cloths and shirts that a man would wear under a coat. This account was found in the Ohio Company Papers at the Historical Society of Pennsylvania.
138. Ibid., 54.
139. Ibid., 55.
140. Ibid., 56. To the author's knowledge, no such list of Trent's men has ever been found.

Chapter 5

141. *Official Records of Robert Dinwiddie*, vol. 1, 73.

142. Ibid., 1–2.

143. George Mason (1725–1792) was a Virginia planter who lived at Gunston Hall near George Washington's Mount Vernon. He was a treasurer for the Ohio Company from 1752 until his death in 1792.

144. Dinwiddie arrived at York in the colonies on November 20, 1751.

145. Dinwiddie's decision to charge one pistole (eighteen shillings) for each land patent to which he attached the royal seal put the House of Burgesses in an uproar since the fee was rarely enforced in Virginia.

146. *Official Records of Robert Dinwiddie*, vol. 1, 45.

147. Ibid., 74.

148. Ibid., 75.

149. Ibid.

150. Ibid.

151. Job Pearsall lived on the south branch of the Potomac River near present-day Romney, West Virginia. It was there that Major James Livingston of the Royal Americans reported to Colonel Henry Bouquet in February 1762 that "[t]he Brass Gun I mentioned in my late Return, I found at a Fort called Pearsals Fort, on the South Branch, with a Quantity of Grape Shot, and 4 Swivels, which they told me belong'd to the Ohio Company."

152. Excerpt from a letter written by William Trent to George Washington dated February 19, 1754. The excerpt appeared in the March 14, 1754 issue of the *Maryland Gazette*.

153. Dejiquequé, or Jesakake, was a Cayuga Indian loyal to the French and had traveled with Washington and Gist from Logstown on November 30, 1753, to see the French commandant at Fort Le Boeuf.

154. *Papiers Contrecoeur*, 105.

155. John Davidson was the Indian interpreter for the Half King and accompanied George Washington to Fort Le Boeuf in November and December 1753.

156. Trent delivered gifts to the Six Nations on July 11, 1753, at Logstown. Listed in his expenses is a payment of six pounds, eleven shillings and four pence to Owens. We can assume that he meant John Owens, who did in fact reside there. H.S.P. Cadwalader Papers, March 1, 1767.

157. Trent arrived at Logstown and spoke to the Half King on July 16, 1753.

158. *Ohio Company Papers*, 25–26.

159. Ibid.

160. *George Mercer Papers Relating to the Ohio Company*, 83.

161. Halfthick was a type of wool.

162. See Governor of Virginia to William Trent, April 8, 1754, State Library of Virginia.

163. Ibid.

164. See Tweedy, *From Beads to Bounty*.

165. *Colonial Records of Pennsylvania*, vol. 6, 195.

166. Neat cattle were animals from the bovine species such as cow or oxen. So, the pistol handles were made from the horns of one of these bovine species.

167. See Governor of Virginia to William Trent, April 8, 1754.

168. Trent's Remarks, 4.

169. Ibid.

170. The Point is now Point State Park, as it was called the Forks of the Ohio and the Mouth of the Monongahela.

171. According to the Privy Council in London, there were two forts proposed to be built. The first was to be built at the mouth of Chartier's Creek and a second built at where the Kanawha River enters into the Ohio River. Ironically, after the Ohio Company changed sites for the fort's location, the Privy Council still assumed in March 1754 that Trent and his men were building at "Shurtees" Creek.

172. *George Mercer Papers Relating to the Ohio Company*, 147–48.

173. A measuring wheel, or "waywiser," as it was commonly known in the eighteenth century, was used to measure distances such as the precise dimensions of a fort.

174. A circumferentor was a surveyor's compass used to calculate horizontal angles, such as the bastions of a proposed fort Trent intended to build for the Ohio Company.

175. Christopher Gist Journals, 34.

176. Trent's Remarks, 4.

177. Ibid.

178. Michel Maray de la Chauvignerie was ensign of the French soldiers, stationed at Logstown in 1754.

179. In English, it meant "Village of the Wolf" and was referring to the Delaware village of Shannopin's Town.

180. *Papiers Contrecoeur*, 108.

181. The "warehouse" they were referring to was the Ohio Company storehouse at the mouth of Redstone Creek.

182. Papiers Contrecoeur, 106.

183. George Washington to James Hamilton, April 24, 1754.

184. Jousts were small beams of timber used to support the door frame.

185. French words meaning "beautiful river" and describing the Ohio River.

186. *Papiers Contrecoeur*, 283.

187. The day Trent says the treaty ended with giving gifts to the Indians in Trent's Remarks, 4.

188. *Official Records of Robert Dinwiddie*, vol. 1, 120.

189. Trent's Remarks, 4.

Chapter 6

190. *Official Records of Robert Dinwiddie*, vol. 1, 92.

191. Ibid.

192. Ibid., 106.

193. The New Store was a two-story warehouse built by the Ohio Company and located on land across the river from present-day Cumberland, Maryland, and known today as Ridgley, West Virginia.

194. Deposition of Edward Ward, 1756, in the *Ohio Company Papers*, 28.

195. A variant of maize that has a strong outer layer hardened like flint.

196. Another variant of maize that has a small indentation at the crown of each kernel.

197. Deposition of Edward Ward, 1756, primarily the Suffering Traders of 1754, 29.

198. Trent's Remarks, 9.

199. *Maryland Gazette*, March 14, 1754.

200. Deposition of Edward Ward, 1756, primarily the Suffering Traders of 1754, 30.

201. Shippen Family Papers, Historical Society of Pennsylvania.

202. Trent's Remarks, 9.

203. Minutes of the Provincial Council, vol. 6, 21.

204. Cadwalader Family Collection, Historical Society of Pennsylvania.

205. Trent's Remarks, 9.

206. Ibid.

207. Trent was talking about ensign Edward Ward and how his lieutenant, John Fraser, had not come down from Turtle Creek.

208. Trent was referring to "one of the storehouses" that Half King had laid the first log and how they were building another building.

209. In *Travels in New France*, the account of a French soldier called "JCB" says the fort was "no more than an enclosure of upright stakes." This has proven to be false.

210. James Foley, an express rider for George Washington, claimed that the distance from Captain Trent's Fort to the Inhabitants was 130 miles. The Papers of George Washington, Colonial Series, vol.1, 83–85.

211. *Ohio Company Papers, 1753–1817*, 29.

212. Trent Remarks, 9.

213. Ibid.

214. *George Mercer Papers Relating to the Ohio Company*, 183.

215. Robert Callender (1726–1776) was an Indian trader from East Pennsboro Township and was one of the "suffering traders" of 1754. Later, he was a colonel in the Cumberland County Militia. He is buried at the Old Graveyard in Carlisle, Pennsylvania.

216. Trent Remarks, 10.

217. James Burd (1725–1793) was a former commander at Fort Augusta and promoted to colonel before the Forbes Expedition to take Fort Duquesne in 1758. He resided in Shippensburg, Pennsylvania, with his wife, Sarah Shippen, to manage his father-in-law Edward Shippen's landholdings.

218. Also spelled Samuel Easdale and Samuel Arsdale. He was an Indian trader from Frederick County and a former employee of the Ohio Company in 1752 and 1753.

219. The letter written by John Davidson to Robert Callender that confirmed the French would be arriving at the Forks of the Ohio in four days.

220. Public Record Office, Colonial Office Class, 5:14, 193–96.

221. Ibid.

222. Ibid.

223. Ibid.

224. *Ohio Company Papers, 1753–1817*, 31.

225. Delaware Indian village located on the Allegheny River just three miles north of the Forks of the Ohio.

226. A pirogue was a long, narrow canoe made from a single tree trunk that could hold up to ten men.

227. A bateau was a flat-bottomed boat that could be anywhere from twenty-four to fifty feet long. It could also mount a small cannon or swivel gun.

228. To strengthen the French claim on the Ohio Valley, the governor of Canada, Roland-Michel Barrin de La Galissonière, ordered Pierre-Joseph

Céloron de Blainville to mark French territory at the mouth of several tributaries by burying lead plates inscribed with the French royal arms to declare the claims of France.

229. Contrecoeur wrote his summons the night before they landed at the Forks of the Ohio at Shannopin's Town on April 16, 1754. Papiers Contrecoeur, 117–19.

Chapter 7

230. The East Pennsboro tract, where Ward and Croghan lived, was located near Silver Spring Township in present-day Mechanicsburg, Pennsylvania, in Cumberland County.

231. PRO Colonial Office, 5:14, 193–96.

232. Ibid.

233. Ibid.

234. Ibid.

235. Samuel Smith was a former sheriff of Lancaster County and was appointed justice of the Court of Common Pleas for the new county of Cumberland on March 10, 1750.

236. *Ohio Company Papers, 1753–1817*, 31.

237. Trent Remarks, 10.

238. Ibid.

239. PRO Colonial Office, 5:14, 193–96.

240. Captain François Le Mercier was second in command and the chief engineer who had built the previous outpost, Fort Le Boeuf.

241. A derogatory term referring to the Seneca and Cayuga, who had bad reputations.

242. An Indian chief ally to the French who lived around present-day Coshocton County, Ohio.

243. PRO Colonial Office, 5:14, 193–96.

244. The French would wave a cloth of the colors of Great Britain, such as red or blue, to parley, while British would use a white color.

245. PRO Colonial Office, 5:14, 193–96.

246. Ibid.

247. John Finley and William Bryan were in partnership with Paul Peirce at the time of their capture on January 28, 1753. *Ohio Company Papers, 1753–1817*, 141.

248. PRO Colonial Office, 5:14, 193–96.

249. Ibid.

250. Ibid.

251. Ibid.

252. The Indians of the Six Nations and Trent's men encamped about three hundred yards from the fort that night.

253. PRO Colonial Office, 5:14, 193–96.

254. Ibid.

255. Michel-Ange Duquesne de Menneville (1700–1778) was a French governor general of New France from 1752 to 1755 and was very aggressive in enforcing French claims in North America.

256. *Papiers Contrecoeur*, 125.

257. John Faulkner was an Indian trader who escaped capture by Indians in January 1753 and lost goods and horses for William Trent when the French took the Forks on April 17, 1754.

258. On January 6, 1754, Washington noted in his journal that seventeen horses were taken by Ohio Company artificers from the Inhabitants to the Forks, and Trent listed on his expense account that he traveled with fourteen more horses when he left the Inhabitants with powder lead and flints for the Indians on January 21. This totals thirty-one horses lost by his hired hand John Faulkner at the Forks when the French came down the Ohio.

259. According to his diary, Washington would get word of Ward's surrender of the Forks on April 19, 1754.

260. PRO Colonial Office, 5:14, 193–96.

261. Ibid.

262. See also Appendix E of David L. Preston's book *Braddock's Defeat*, 351, and the full account of this unnamed Ohio Iroquois warrior's account at Will's Creek that Preston discovered researching at the National Archives of the United Kingdom.

263. James Innes (1700–1759) was a veteran officer of the War for Jenkin's Ear and served as the succeeding commander of all colonial soldiers in the Ohio Country in 1754 after the unfortunate death of Colonel Joshua Fry.

264. PRO Colonial Office, 5:15, 194–95.

Chapter 8

265. Near present-day Clairton, Pennsylvania.

266. A gentleman justice or justice of the peace was unpaid, but the position was taken up usually by a landed gentleman of high standing in the community and living within proximity to the local court.

267. Minutes of the Court of Yohogania County, Virginia, October 26, 1779, Annuals of the Carnegie Museum, vol. 2, 2 and 372.

268. *Papers of Henry Bouquet*, vol. 2, 546.

269. Bouquet's breastworks was located about one mile north of Turtle Creek, about eight miles from the Forks of the Ohio and Fort Duquesne.

270. *Diaries of George Washington*, 177.

271. Joshua Fry (1699–1754) was a member of the House of Burgesses and an influential Virginia mapmaker along with Peter Jefferson. He was a professor of mathematics and natural philosophy at the College of William and Mary and the commander of all the colonial forces, including the Virginia Regiment in 1754.

272. *Diaries of George Washington*, 177.

273. Ibid., 177–78.

274. Ibid., 180.

275. Ibid.

276. Elizabeth Williams was only known confirmed woman trader in Pennsylvania.

277. Andrew McBriar was an Indian trader who on June 21, 1752, narrowly escaped Pickawillany with Thomas Burney after French and Indians burned the fort and killed the Piankashaw chief "Old Briton."

278. Steele, *Setting All the Captives Free*, 51, 91–92.

279. *Official Records of Robert Dinwiddie*, vol. 1, 170.

280. Ibid.

281. *Diaries of George Washington*, 182. The standard rate for volunteers and first raised troops was two shillings per day. The rate for a private soldier was only eight pence per day, three times less than a volunteer.

282. There are twelve pence in a shilling, so two shillings a day was equivalent to twenty-four pence per day.

283. Clark, *Colonial Soldiers of the South*, 484.

284. *Journal of Colonel George Washington Commanding a Detachment of Virginia*, 181.

285. Ibid.

286. Ibid., 181.

287. *Official Records of Robert Dinwiddie*, vol. 1, 147.

288. Ibid., 149.

289. Colonel Joshua Fry sustained mortal wounds after a fall from his horse just outside Will's Creek on May 31, 1754.
290. *Official Records of Robert Dinwiddie*, vol. 1, 461.
291. Ibid., 288–89.
292. *Ohio Company Papers, 1753–1817*, 347–48.

Chapter 9

293. *Official Records of Robert Dinwiddie*, vol. 1, 170.
294. Trent Remarks, 9.
295. *George Mercer Papers Relating to the Ohio Company*, 571.
296. Ibid., 570.
297. Shippen Family Papers XV, 119, Historical Society of Pennsylvania.
298. *Ohio Company Papers, 1753–1817*, 30.
299. *Official Records of Robert Dinwiddie*, vol. 1, 112.
300. James, *Ohio Company*, 239; George Mason to Colonel James Tilghman, March 1, 1767, Cadwalader Papers, Historical Society of Pennsylvania.
301. *Official Records of Robert Dinwiddie*, vol. 1, 114.
302. *George Mercer Papers Relating to the Ohio Company*, 83.
303. George Mason to Colonel James Tilghman, March 1, 1767, Cadwalader Papers, Historical Society of Pennsylvania.
304. James, *Ohio Company*, 240.
305. John Mercer (1704–1768) was a leading Virginia attorney and colonial prosecutor for the King's Court of Virginia; he was also the secretary and general counsel for the Ohio Company.
306. *Official Records of Robert Dinwiddie*, vol. 2, 703 and 718.
307. *Ohio Company Papers, 1753–1817*, 347–48.
308. Ibid.
309. James, *Ohio Company*, 230–32.
310. A "tithable" person was any free Caucasian male over age of sixteen, all "Negros" imported whether male or female and Indian servants' whether male or female (however procured) being sixteen years of age. Adult white women would not be included unless head of the household.
311. *Journals of the House of Burgesses of Virginia, 1758–1761*, 255.
312. Ibid.
313. Ibid.

Chapter 10

314. *Legislative Journals of the Council of Colonial Virginia*, vol. 3 (1754–1775), 1,133.

315. John Campbell, 4th Earl of Loudon (1705–1782), was the commander in chief and governor general of Virginia in 1756. He was later replaced by James Abercromby.

316. On December 11, 1753, Major George Washington arrived at Fort Le Boeuf and delivered a letter from Governor Dinwiddie to the French commandant, General Jacques Legardeur de Saint-Pierre, asking the French to return to Canada.

317. This "private company" Washington was referring to was the Ohio Company.

318. *Official Records of Robert Dinwiddie*, vol. 1, 171.

319. Winchester, Virginia, was about 60 miles from the Ohio Company warehouse at the New Store, then about 70 miles to the mouth of the Redstone Creek, 29 miles to John Fraser's cabin at Turtle Creek and finally 8 miles to the Forks of the Ohio. Almost 170 miles in the dead of winter.

320. Charles M. Stotz, an architectural historian, wrote a remarkable book titled *Outposts of the War for Empire* that goes into vivid detail of the British and French outposts during the French and Indian War.

321. William A. Hunter authored the book *Forts on the Pennsylvania Frontier 1753–1758*.

322. Like the Redstone Creek storehouse.

323. *Pennsylvania Archives*, vol. 2, 238.

324. The Papers of George Washington, Colonial Series, vol.1, 83–85.

325. Horace Walpole (1717–1797) was an English art historian and a member of Parliament. He is remembered today as one of the most assiduous letter writers of the English language.

326. *Official Records of Robert Dinwiddie*, vol. 1, 343.

327. An indemnity bond is coverage for the loss of an oblige when a principal fails to perform according to the terms agreed on between the obligee and the principal.

328. James Tilghman (1716–1793) was a prominent lawyer in Maryland and Pennsylvania and for the Ohio Company.

329. Thomas Cresap to James Tilghman, May 20, 1767, Historical Society of Pennsylvania.

330. Ibid.

331. A person who travels from place to place to deliver letters.

332. Cresap delivered the commission personally to William Trent on February 10, 1754, at Redstone Creek.

333. Trent's father, William, was a devout member and vestryman of Christ Church in Philadelphia from 1715 to 1720, a trait his son seemed to follow later in his adult life. Not only did Trent manage to baptize all six of his children in the Church of England throughout his various residences from 1754 to 1768, but like his father, he also became a vestryman, for St. Michael's Episcopal Church in Trenton, New Jersey, on January 4, 1783.

334. The advertisement for the apprehension of Trent's deserters was found in the *Pennsylvania Gazette* issue of August 7, 1746.

335. At the corner of Arch and Second Street in Philadelphia was George Tavern, and there stood a sign known as "Sign of St George or Sign of the George." It was a frequent meeting spot for both tavern dwellers and wayside travelers in the city.

336. Benjamin Franklin (1706–1790) was one of the Founding Fathers of the United States, as well as a renowned author, scientist and newspaper editor for the *Pennsylvania Gazette*.

337. Richard Partridge (1681–1759) was the official colonial agent and representative for Pennsylvania and resided in London.

338. Supposedly said by Benjamin Franklin to the Continental Congress.

Epilogue

339. "Braddock's Field" or near present-day North Braddock, Pennsylvania, where the battle took place.

340. John Forbes (1707–1759) was a British officer promoted to brigadier general and ordered to lead an expedition in 1758 to take Fort Duquesne. He was successful and renamed the Forks of the Ohio "Pittsbourg."

341. William Pitt the Elder, 1st Earl of Chatham (1708–1778), was a British statesman of the Whig group and the secretary of state who provided funding to seek whatever was necessary to defeat the French in North America.

342. Ward was a captain in the First Pennsylvania Battalion under Lieutenant Colonel Hugh Mercer during the Forbes Expedition of 1758.

343. The superintendent of Indian affairs was William Johnson.

344. The Huron nation were also known as the Wyandots.

345. *Papers of Henry Bouquet*, vol. 4, 407–11.

346. William Clapham (1722–1763) was an officer in the Third Battalion of Pennsylvania and, while out scouting away from Fort Pitt, was killed near the mouth of Sewickley Creek on May 28, 1763.

347. The Wolfe was also known by his Delaware name, Kikyuscung.

348. William Trent's Journal at Fort Pitt 1763, Historical Society of Pennsylvania.

349. Fort Sandusky was a British military fort from 1761 to 1763.

350. Turtle's Heart, or Turtleheart, was a Delaware warrior who lived at the village of Shaningo, near the tributaries of Big Beaver Creek.

351. Alexander McKee (1735–1799) was a fur trader and Indian interpreter at Fort Pitt. His eventual land grant is where the borough of McKee's Rocks lies today.

352. William Trent's Journal of Fort Pitt, 1763, Historical Society of Pennsylvania.

353. The commander of Fort Pitt was Swiss-born Simeon Ecuyer.

354. It was apparent that Ecuyer and Trent were hoping to decimate the native population by means of biological warfare. There is little specific evidence that exists, if any at all, that the blankets did indeed have a "desirous effect." William Trent's Journal of Fort Pitt, 1763, Historical Society of Pennsylvania.

355. Pontiac's War, or Pontiac's Uprising, was named after Ottawa chief Pontiac and the tribes in the Ohio Valley and Great Lakes region, who were upset with British occupation on their lands after the French and Indian War ended.

356. The new colony would have been an expansion of the Indiana grant that was promised to them after the Treaty of Stanwix in 1768 and would be today southwestern Pennsylvania, West Virginia and parts of Kentucky. The proposed name, Vandalia, was in honor of the wife of King George III, Charlotte of Mecklenburg-Streliz, who was descended from Vandalic tribesmen.

357. After Pontiac's War, the British turned Fort Pitt over to the colonists. When the Virginians took control of it, they renamed it Fort Dunmore after Lord John Murray, 4th Earl of Dunmore, and governor of Virginia.

358. No such letters in Trent's handwriting have ever been found dated past his own will of July 6, 1784. In the Clifford-Pemberton Papers of the Historical Society of Pennsylvania, Thomas Clifford of Philadelphia wrote to Anthony Todd of London on December 27, 1784 that "[a] bout the first instant, William Trent Departed this life he made a Will appointed Saml. Wharton John Todd Junr and Others his executors was

I believe very low in Circumstances having been helped in his Last Illness for sometime Past by his Friends."

359. Since Trent was living with family or friends when he died in Philadelphia in December 1784, it is observed by Thomas Clifford's letter that Trent's lands and assets were still being sorted out. It is also assumed that his wife, Sarah, couldn't afford a proper burial for Trent, since no newspaper in Pennsylvania or New Jersey in 1784 or early 1785 gives mention of his passing. Then it can be assumed that Trent was probably laid to rest discreetly nearby in a potter's field like Washington Square, where former military soldiers and paupers were wrapped in a shroud and put in an unmarked grave. His exact burial remains unknown.

360. Trent Street lies in the Hill District of Pittsburgh, Pennsylvania.

Biographical Sketch of William Trent

361. The exact year of birth for William Trent is a matter for debate, as is his birthplace since his father, William, and mother, Mary, were residing in the city of Philadelphia during the supposed birth year in question, 1715, including at a "country house" in Passyunk Township. However, since he was still working as an apprentice under Edward Shippen in 1742 and 1743, it is rather doubtful that the birth year of 1715 (theorized by most historians) was correct due to the Pennsylvania law for a merchant's apprenticeship that stated that anyone learning a trade such as Trent was bound to his master until he had turned the age of twenty-one. In 1742, then, in accordance to that birth year, he would have been twenty-seven and too old to still be an apprentice. Therefore, a more accurate birth year would list him being born around 1721 or 1722 and residing at the house his father built on Assunpink Creek in Trenton, New Jersey.

362. James Trent (1699–July 23, 1734) was the son of William Trent and his first wife, Mary Burge, and was born at their residence on Front Street in Philadelphia. He was the eldest half brother of William Trent and was educated at St. Peters College, an independent grammar school in Westminster Abbey, and later at the Middle Temple and Balliol College in 1717. He was married to Elizabeth Willbee at the Lincoln's Inn Chapel on January 17, 1724. Later, he conducted the inventory for his deceased father's estate, was a prosperous merchant in Trenton and owned the William Trent House from 1724 to 1729.

363. The Queen's Scholar program, originally founded in 1560 by Queen Elizabeth I, awarded scholarships to those exclusively selected to Westminster School, located in Westminster Abbey in London. James Trent was selected at age fourteen in 1714, and because of his exclusive selection, he was allowed with other fellow scholars to attend the coronation of George Ludwig (King George I) on October 20, 1714.

364. Westminster School Archives and Records, London.

365. The mouth of Conococheague Creek empties into the Potomac River near present-day Williamsport, Maryland.

366. Trent was commissioned a major according to a letter dated June 2, 1763, that was written to Colonel Henry Bouquet from Fort Pitt commander Simeon Ecuyer.

367. Located on present-day Fourth and Market Streets in Philadelphia, it was run at the time by innkeeper Francis Lee.

368. In the New Jersey State Archives, there is a four-page document about William Trent issuing his power of attorney on June 1, 1784, to Elijah Bond of Trenton to "take and Receive Peaceable and Quiet possession and Seizin of and in all and singular the Lands" as he was now at present in Philadelphia.

369. We know now for the first time from the December 27, 1784 letter written to Anthony Todd from Thomas Clifford that William Trent died on December 1, 1784.

BIBLIOGRAPHY

Manuscript Collections

American Philosophical Society, Philadelphia
    Burd-Shippen Papers
Historical Society of Pennsylvania, Philadelphia
    Cadwalader Family Papers, 1623–1962
    Clifford-Pemberton Papers
    Etting Collection–Ohio Company Papers
    James Hamilton Papers
    Shippen Family Papers
    William Trent Fort Pitt Journal, 1763
Library of Congress, Washington, D.C.
    Shippen Family Papers, 1671–1936 (microfilm)
Library of Virginia, Richmond
    Colonial Papers, 1630–1778 (microfilm)
Maryland State Archives, Annapolis
    Maryland Gazette, 1728–1839 (microfilm)
National Archives (UK)
    Colonial Office Papers (CO), Class 5 Files, Parts 1–4 (microfilm)
New Jersey Historical Society
    New Jersey Manuscript Collection, 1669–1840
New York Historical Society
    Colden Cadwallader Papers, 1711–75

University of Delaware Special Collections
  The Accounts of Benjamin Franklin through 1747
University of Pittsburgh Archives Service Center, Pittsburgh
  Burd-Shippen Family Papers, 1717–1898
  Darlington Family Papers, 1753–1921
William L. Clements Library, University of Michigan, Ann Arbor
  William Trent Manuscript, 1757, Native American History Collection

Selected Primary Sources

Bailey, Kenneth P., ed. *The Ohio Company Papers, 1753–1817: Being Primarily Papers of the Suffering Traders of Pennsylvania.* Arcata, CA, 1947.

Brock, Robert Alonzo, ed. *The Official Records of Robert Dinwiddie.* 2 vols. Richmond: Virginia Historical Society, 1883–84.

Clark, Murtie June, ed. *Colonial Soldiers of the South, 1732–1774.* Baltimore, MD: Genealogical Publishing Company, 1983.

Darlington, Mary C., ed. *History of Colonel Henry Bouquet and the Western Frontiers of Pennsylvania, 1747–1764.* Pittsburgh, PA: University of Pittsburgh Press, 1920.

Darlington, William M., ed. *Christopher Gist Journals.* Pittsburgh, PA: J.R. Weldin and Company, 1893.

Goodman, Alfred T., ed. *Journal of Captain William Trent from Logstown to Pickawillany A.D. 1752.* Cincinnati, OH: William Dodge, 1871.

Grenier, Fernand, ed. *Papiers Contrecoeur et Autres Documents Concernant le Conflit Anglo-Francais sur l'Ohio de 1745 à 1756.* Québec: Les Presses Universitaires Laval, 1952.

Hall, Wilmer L., ed. *Executive Journals of the Council of Colonial Virginia.* Vol. 5, *1739–1754.* Richmond: Virginia State Library, 1945.

Hazard, Samuel, ed. *Pennsylvania Archives.* 12 vols. Philadelphia, PA: Joseph Severns, 1852.

Jackson, Donald, and Dorothy Twohig, eds. *The Diaries of George Washington.* 5 vols. Charlottesville: University of Virginia, 1978.

McIlwaine, H.R., ed. *Journals of the House of Burgesses of Virginia, 1758–1761.* Richmond: Virginia State Library, 1908.

———. *Legislative Journals of the Council of Colonial Virginia.* Vol. 3. Richmond: Virginia State Library, 1919.

Moon, Robert Charles, ed. *The Morris Family of Philadelphia, Descendants of Anthony Morris, Born 1654–1721 Died.* 4 vols. Philadelphia, PA: Robert C. Moon, 1898.

Mulkearn, Lois, ed. *George Mercer Papers Relating to the Ohio Company of Virginia.* Pittsburgh, PA: University of Pittsburgh Press, 1954.

Munro, James, ed. *Acts of the Privy Council of England, Colonial Series.* Vol. 4, *1745–1766.* London: His Majesty's Stationery Office, 1911.

Paltsits, Victor Hugo, ed. *A Narrative of the Captivity of Nehemiah How in 1745–1747* Boston: Burrows Brother Company, 1904.

Rutland, Robert A., ed. *The Papers of George Mason, 1725–1792.* 3 vols. Chapel Hill: University of North Carolina Press, 1970.

Scott, Kenneth., ed. *Abstracts of Pennsylvania Gazette, 1728–1748.* Baltimore, MD: Genealogical Publishing Company, 1975.

Stevens, Sylvester K., Donald H. Kent and Louis M. Waddell, eds. *The Papers of Henry Bouquet.* 6 vols. Harrisburg: Pennsylvania Historical Commission, 1941.

Toner, Joseph M., ed. *Journal of Colonel George Washington Commanding a Detachment of Virginia Troops.* Albany, NY: Joel Munsell's Sons Publishers, 1893.

Selected Secondary Sources

Alexander, Philip. *Virginia Magazine of History and Biography.* Richmond: Virginia Historical Society, 1893.

Bailey, Kenneth P. *Christopher Gist: Colonial Frontiersman, Explorer, and Indian Agent.* Hamden, CT: Archon Books, 1976.

Fleming, George T. *History of Pittsburgh and Environs.* New York: American Historical Society Inc., 1922.

Hunter, William A. *Forts on the Pennsylvania Frontier, 1753–1758.* Harrisburg: Pennsylvania Historical and Museum Commission, 1960.

James, Alfred P. *The Ohio Company: Its Inner History.* Pittsburgh, PA: University of Pittsburgh Press, 1959.

MacGregor, Doug. "The Shot Not Heard Around the World: Trent's Fort and the Opening of the War for Empire." *Pennsylvania History* 74, no. 3 (2007).

Preston, David L. *Braddock's Defeat: The Battle of the Monongahela and the Road to Revolution.* New York: Oxford University Press, 2015.

Sipe, C. Hale. *The Indian Wars of Pennsylvania.* Harrisburg, PA: Telegraph Press, 1929.

Slick, Sewell E. *William Trent and the West.* Harrisburg, PA: Archives Publishing Company, 1947.

Steele, Ian. *Setting All the Captives Free: Capture, Adjustment, and Recollection in Allegheny Country.* Montreal: Queens-McGill, 2013.

Stotz, Charles M. *Outposts of the War for Empire: The French and English in Western Pennsylvania: Their Armies, Their Forts, Their People, 1749–1764.* Pittsburgh: Historical Society of Western Pennsylvania, 1985.

Tweedy, Ann C. *From Beads to Bounty: How Wampum Became America's First Currency—and Lost Its Power.* Washington, D.C.: Indian Country Today Media Network, 2017.

Wainwright, Nicholas B. *George Croghan: Wilderness Diplomat.* Chapel Hill: University of North Carolina Press, 1959.

Wallace, Paul A.W. *Indian Paths of Pennsylvania.* Harrisburg: Pennsylvania Historical and Museum Commission, 1965.

INDEX

ABOUT THE AUTHOR

J ason A. Cherry has lived in Western Pennsylvania his entire life and has interpreted the French and Indian War for almost thirty years. He resides in Butler, Pennsylvania, in the heart of the Ohio Country with his wife, Emily, and his two daughters, Penny and Charlotte.

Visit us at
www.historypress.com